PERSIAN Myths

Author's note and acknowledgements

This book is not intended to be a complete and detailed view of all known Persian myths, and undoubtedly many other stories could have been included instead. The choice is personal and subjective, and it has been made primarily to show the importance and continuity of Persian myths from ancient times into the Islamic period.

No standard system of transliteration has been used for personal and place names, but they have been presented in the way most familiar to English readers without using diacritics. Passages quoted in English translation are from J. Darmesteter, *The Zend-Avesta*; E. W. West, *The Pahlavi Texts (Bundahishn)*; A. G. and E. Warner, *The Shahnama of Firdausi*; E. W. Lane, *The Arabian Night's Entertainments*; and E. G. Browne, *A Literary History of Persia* (vol. 1). Shorter translations from the *Shahnameh, Vis and Ramin, Iskandarnameh*, and *Khusrow and Shirin* that appear within the body of the text have been made by the author from the original Persian. More detailed references to published material for further reading can be found on p. 79.

Finally, I am most grateful to the Department of Western Asiatic Antiquities and Oriental Antiquities of the British Museum for allowing me to browse through their photographic archives, to Dr Sheila Canby for advice on Persian miniatures, to Miss Ann Searight for drawing the map, and to all those who supported and encouraged me in writing this book; in particular I should like to mention Nina Shandloff, who has edited and seen it through the press.

Above all, my sincere thanks go to my family and my husband, John Curtis, for their support.

PERSIAN
Myths

VESTA SARKHOSH CURTIS

Orient BlackSwan

ORIENT BLACKSWAN PRIVATE LIMITED

Registered Office
3-6-752 Himayatnagar, Hyderabad 500 029 (A.P.), India
Email: centraloffice@orientblackswan.com

Other Offices
Bangalore, Bhopal, Bhubaneshwar, Chandigarh, Chennai
Ernakulam, Guwahati, Hyderabad, Jaipur
Kolkata, Lucknow, Mumbai, New Delhi, Noida, Patna, Pune

Reprinted 2005, 2006, 2009

Published by The British Museum Press
A division of The British Museum Company Ltd
38 Russell Square, London WC1B 3QQ

Published in India by
Orient Blackswan Private Limited 2010

ISBN 978 81 250 3949 5

Printed in India at
Aegean Offset Printers
Greater Noida

Published by
Orient Blackswan Private Limited
1/24 Asaf Ali Road, New Delhi 110 002
Email: delhi@orientblackswan.com

Designed by Gill Monqué and Diane Butler
Cover design by Jim Stanton

FRONT COVER: 'Rustam Kills the Dragon', from a *Shahnameh*, Qazvin, c. 984-5/1576–7, ascribed to Sadiqi Beg, opaque watercolour, gold and ink on paper. Reproduced by kind permission of the Collection of the Aga Khan.

THIS PAGE: *View of Mt Demavand in the Alburz Mountains, north of Tehran, with the Lar Valley in the foreground.*

Contents

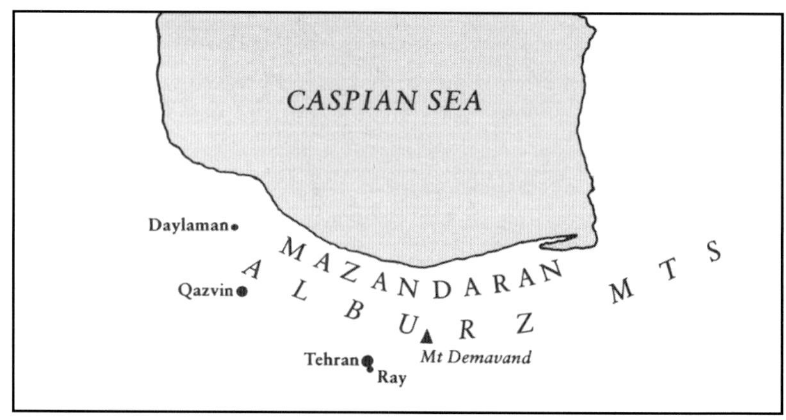

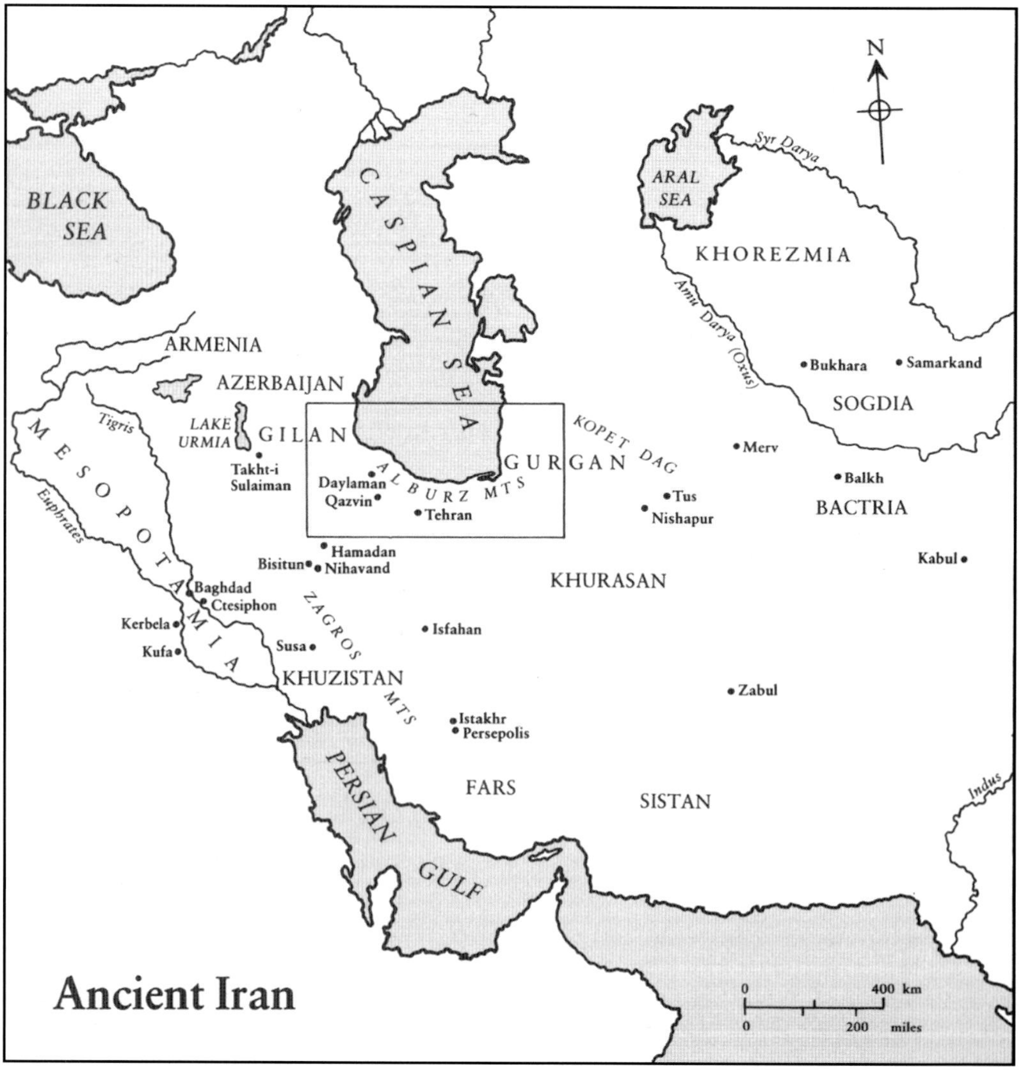

CASPIAN SEA
Daylaman
Qazvin
MAZANDARAN
ALBURZ MTS
Mt Demavand
Tehran
Ray

N
BLACK SEA
CASPIAN SEA
ARAL SEA
Syr Darya
KHOREZMIA
Amu Darya (Oxus)
ARMENIA
AZERBAIJAN
LAKE URMIA
GILAN
Tigris
MESOPOTAMIA
Euphrates
Takht-i Sulaiman
Daylaman
Qazvin
ALBURZ MTS
Tehran
GURGAN
KOPET DAG
Merv
Bukhara
Samarkand
SOGDIA
Balkh
BACTRIA
Tus
Nishapur
Hamadan
Bisitun
Nihavand
Kabul
KHURASAN
Baghdad
Ctesiphon
Kerbela
Kufa
ZAGROS MTS
Susa
Isfahan
KHUZISTAN
Zabul
Istakhr
Persepolis
PERSIAN GULF
FARS
SISTAN
Indus
0 400 km
0 200 miles

Ancient Iran

Introduction

Persian myths are traditional tales and stories of ancient origin, some involving extraordinary or supernatural beings. Drawn from the legendary past of Iran, they reflect the attitudes of the society to which they first belonged – attitudes towards the confrontation of good and evil, the actions of the gods, and the exploits of heroes and fabulous creatures. Myths play a crucial part in Persian culture and our understanding of them is increased when we consider them within the context of Iranian history.

For this purpose we must ignore modern political boundaries and look at historical developments in greater Iran, a vast area covering parts of Central Asia well beyond the frontiers of present-day Iran. The geography of this region, with its high mountain ranges, plays a significant role in many of the mythological stories. Although the archaeological record shows that civilis-ation in Iran dates from before 6000 BC, it is only the period from *c.* 2000 BC onwards that is of interest to us here. The second millennium is usually regarded as the age of migration because the emergence in western Iran of a new form of pottery, similar to earlier wares of north-eastern Iran, suggests the arrival of new people. This pottery, light grey to black in colour, appeared around 1400 BC. It is called Early Grey Ware or Iron I, the latter name indicating the beginning of the Iron Age in this area.

The migration of Iranian-speaking peoples into Iran is a widely discussed issue, and many questions about how the migration took place remain unanswered. Certainly there was a break in tradition at sites on the southern slopes of the Alburz Mountains and in western Iran, where stone tombs were filled with rich grave goods. On the basis of linguistic evidence, these newly arrived peoples are regarded as having originally been among the Indo-Iranians who for a long period shared a common tradition while living as nomads in the Asian steppes of Russia. Eventually the two linguistically related groups separated and migrated southwards. By the middle of the second millennium BC, the Iranian group had moved into the highlands of Iran through the flat passable area south-east of the Caspian Sea, while the Indian tribes had migrated into the Indian sub-continent. Whether the migration was violent and whether the tribes moved in large groups are questions that cannot be answered with certainty. One can only see from the archaeological evidence a break from the previous traditions and the arrival of new pottery types and burial rites. Nor do we know what happened to the language of the indigenous population, which in most parts of the country was replaced by the Iranian languages of the newcomers.

The first definite mention of an Iranian tribe, the Medes, occurs in ninth-century BC Assyrian texts. The Medes became the main threat to the Assyrian empire in the east. Whereas at first the Medes were only a loose confederation of tribes, by the late seventh century BC they had become powerful enough to join forces with the Babylonians and cause the collapse of the Assyrian empire in 612 BC. Another Iranian group, the Persians, had settled in southern Iran, in the area of Fars. It was through the amalgamation of the related tribes of the Medes and the Persians under Cyrus the Great that the Achaemenid empire was formed, emerging as the dominant power in the ancient Near East from *c.* 550 until its conquest by Alexander the Great in 331 BC.

The period of foreign rule by Alexander and his Greek generals, the Seleucids, was brief. Then the Arsacid Parthians, originally an Iranian-speaking nomadic group from the north-east, moved into the area south-east of the Caspian Sea. Under their king Arsaces I, they moved into Seleucid territory and established Parthian rule in 238 BC. By 141 BC the Parthians had conquered Mesopotamia under their great ruler, Mithradates I, and for the next three and a half centuries they remained the major political force in the ancient Near East and the main opponents of the Romans. Under Mithradates II (known as the Great), the Parthian empire stretched from the River Euphrates in the west to eastern Iran and Central Asia.

The dynasty of the Parthians came to an end in AD 224 with the defeat of their last king, Artabanus IV/V, by Ardashir I. The latter was a local prince, from Istakhr near Persepolis, who had received his crown from the Parthian monarch and later successfully challenged him. With his victory, Ardashir established the dynasty of the Sasanians, named after their legendary ancestor Sasan. The eventual collapse of the Sasanians was due to the rise of Islam and the Arab conquest of Iran in AD 642, by which time their army and treasury had been exhausted by numerous wars and the population could no longer endure the high taxes imposed on them. Zoroastrianism, the official state religion of Iran under the Sasanians, was replaced by Islam.

Much of our information about the ancient Iranians, their gods and the creation of their world can be found in the religious texts of the Zoroastrians, whose prophet Zoroaster (Greek for Persian Zarathushtra) may have lived in Khorezmia in Central Asia, or even further north-east. His dates are much debated and far from certain, but linguistic evidence from the *Gatha*, the prophet's hymns, in a part of the *Avesta*, the holy book of the Zoroastrians, suggests a close link with the ancient Indian hymns, the *Rigveda* of *c.* 1700 BC. This is the period prior to the migration of nomadic tribes into Iran and India. The original *Avesta*, written in Avestan, an east-Iranian language, dates from between 1400 and 1200 BC, and Zoroaster himself probably lived around 1000 BC. Some scholars favour a date in the late seventh and early sixth century BC for Zoroaster, but this is less likely.

The holy book of the Zoroastrians was memorised by Zoroastrian priests and passed on by word of mouth over a long period of time. Later sources claim that the *Avesta* was originally written in gold on prepared ox-hides and stored at

Bronze belt plaque of the Parthian period, probably 2nd–early 3rd century AD*, showing a bearded rider and his horse. Elaborate belt plaques are common in this period and the rider figure is depicted with the typical bushy hairstyle, headband and outfit of the time, consisting of tunic and trousers.*

Istakhr, and that it was destroyed by Alexander. Although parts of the sacred text are assumed to have been written down again during the Parthian period, in the first and second centuries AD, the *Avesta* did not exist in its complete form until perhaps the sixth century AD, under the Sasanians. Unfortunately, this version has not survived. The present *Avesta* dates back to the thirteenth or fourteenth century and contains only a fraction of the original. It is divided into sections: the *Yasna*, which is a collection of prayers and contains the *Gatha* (the hymns of the prophet Zoroaster); the *Visparad*; the *Vendidad* (also known as the *Videvdat*), the 'Law against Demons'; the *Small Avesta* (*Khurdeh Avesta*); and the *Yasht* or hymns, in which many pagan myths of pre-Zoroastrian origin are described.

The *Avesta* was first translated into a Western language in 1771 by a Frenchman, Anquetil du Perron. This much-criticised French version was followed by a series of translations, although the first English edition, by James Darmesteter, was not published until 1887.

The myths which appear in the part of the *Avesta* known as *Yasht* include some tales of very ancient pre-Zoroastrian origin, probably belonging to the pagan Indo-Iranian era. They describe the heroic deeds performed by gods, kings and warriors against both supernatural and human enemies. Many of these myths reappear in the *Shahnameh (Book of Kings)*, an epic in rhyme by the poet Firdowsi, which was completed in AD 1010. Books about the history of the past had previously appeared in the Sasanian period and during the rule of the Abbasid caliphs in the eighth century AD many of these books were translated from Pahlavi (Middle Persian) into Arabic, although in most cases both the original Pahlavi texts and the Arabic translations have been lost. However, writers such as Firdowsi, who were well acquainted with the earlier literature, ensured its survival. Thus written sources, together with a strong oral tradition, have kept the myths and stories of Persia alive down to the present. Their importance and relevance to modern Persian society lies in the fact that most Iranians, whether literate or not, know something about these stories. The *Shahnameh* in particular plays a crucial role in Persian life and culture, not only because of its considerable literary merit but also because of its importance in preserving the myths and history of a very distant past in the Persian language.

The gods and the creation of the ancient Iranian world

Much information about the ancient Iranians, their gods and the creation of their world can be found in the religious texts of the Zoroastrians, which include the *Avesta* and later sources such as the *Bundahishn* and *Denkard*. The *Bundahishn* or 'Creation' consists of Pahlavi (Middle Persian) translations of parts of the *Avesta* that no longer exist and their commentaries (*Zand*). The *Denkard* gives a summary of the *Avesta* in Pahlavi.

Within the *Avesta*, the gods, heroes and fabulous creatures mostly appear in the section known as the *Yasht*. Here, myths of pre-Zoroastrian origin which reflect a pagan ideology are described in hymns dedicated to various gods. For example, *Yasht* 5 (or *Aban Yasht*) is dedicated to the goddess Ardvi Sura Anahita; *Yasht* 14, also known as *Bahram Yasht*, is dedicated to the god Verethragna, and *Yasht* 10, the *Mihr Yasht*, describes the god Mithra. *Yasht* 19 (*Zamyad Yasht*) gives a description of the quest for the Divine Glory. Also informative is the collection of prayers, the *Niyayesh*, which incorporates early Zoroastrian beliefs. These include the *Atash Niyayesh*, a prayer to Fire. The *Vendidad* deals with the creations of Ahura Mazda, the Wise Lord, and the destruction wrought by his opponent, Angra Mainyu, known in later times as Ahriman.

Gods

Ahura Mazda and Angra Mainyu

Ahura Mazda, the Wise Lord, is the ultimate God, the absolute goodness, wisdom and knowledge, creator of the sun, the stars, light and dark, humans and animals and all spiritual and physical activities. He is opposed to all evil and suffering. In opposition to him is Angra Mainyu (Ahriman), the Evil Spirit, who is constantly attempting to destroy the world of truth and to harm men and beasts. Thus life in this world is a reflection of the cosmic struggle between Ahura Mazda and Angra Mainyu. Zoroaster's teaching says that Ahura Mazda personifies goodness and that all human beings must choose between good and evil. The arch-demon Angra Mainyu lives in darkness in the north, the home of all demons, and he is capable of changing his appearance to that of a lizard, a snake or a youth. So disguised, he fights all that is good and attempts to lure all,

Bronze winged demon with lion's body and ferocious head, perhaps representing the Evil Spirit. Allegedly found in Afghanistan. Late Sasanian/early Islamic, 7th–8th century AD.

even Zoroaster himself, into his world of darkness, deceit and lies. In his continuous battle against good, including the creations of Ahura Mazda, he is assisted by a number of other demons. The most important of these is Aeshma, the demon of fury and outrage, and Azhi Dahaka, the monster with three heads, six eyes and three jaws, whose body is full of lizards and scorpions. According to Zoroastrian texts, Angra Mainyu will be defeated at the end of the world.

Ardvi Sura Anahita

Ardvi Sura Anahita is the goddess of all the waters upon the earth and the source of the cosmic ocean. She drives a chariot pulled by four horses: wind, rain, cloud and sleet. She is regarded as the source of life, purifying the seed of all males and the wombs of all females, and cleansing the milk in the breasts of all mothers. Because of her connection with life, warriors in battle prayed to her for survival and victory. The *Aban Yasht* is dedicated to her and describes her descent to the earth thus:

> Then Ardvi Sura Anahita came forth, O Zarathustra! down from those stars to the earth made by Mazda . . .
> (*Yasht* 5, 88)

When asked by Zoroaster how she should be worshipped, the goddess replies:

> O pure, holy Spitama! . . . this is the sacrifice wherewith thou shalt worship and forward me, from the time when the sun is rising to the time when the sun is setting. Of this libation of mine thou shalt drink . . .
> (*Yasht* 5, 91)

In a vivid description, Ardvi Sura Anahita is compared to a fair maid with a strong body, tall, pure and

> nobly born of a glorious race, wearing . . . a mantle fully embroidered with gold; ever holding the baresma [barsom = bundle of consecrated twigs] in her hand, according to the rules, she wears square golden earrings . . . and a golden necklace . . . Upon her head Ardvi Sura Anahita bound a golden crown, with a hundred stars, with eight rays . . . a well-made crown . . . with fillets streaming down.
> (*Yasht* 5, 126–8)

Anahita is worshipped by heroes and anti-heroes alike in the *Avesta*, who pray to her and offer sacrifices. The important status of this goddess is best seen in the struggle between good and evil and the confrontation between the kings of Iran and the rulers of Turya (Turan), the area to the north-east of Iran.

Verethragna

Verethragna is the warrior god, the aggressive, victorious force against evil. In the *Bahram Yasht*, a hymn dedicated to him, he takes the ten different forms of a strong wind, a bull with yellow ears and golden horns, a white horse with golden trappings, a burden-bearing camel, a male boar, a youth at the ideal age of fifteen, a swift bird (perhaps a raven), a wild ram, a fighting deer, and a man holding a sword with a golden blade. When Zoroaster asks Ahura Mazda what to do if affected by the curse of the enemy, the Wise Lord instructs him to take a feather of Verethragna, incarnated as a bird:

> With that feather thou shalt rub thy own body, with that feather thou shalt curse back the enemies. If a man holds a bone of that strong bird, no one can smite or turn to flight that fortunate man. The feather of that bird brings him help.
> (*Yasht* 14, 35–6)

There is an interesting parallel here with the story of the Simurgh in the *Shahnameh*, whose feathers also have a healing effect. Verethragna is also reported to carry

> the chariots of the lords . . . the chariots of the sovereigns.
> (*Yasht* 14, 39)

In a description of the god Mithra, Verethragna is mentioned as the one who

> . . . made by Ahura, runs opposing the foes in the shape of a boar, a sharp-toothed he-boar, a sharp-jawed boar, that kills at one stroke, pursuing, wrathful, with a dripping face; strong, with iron feet, iron fore-paws, iron weapons, an iron tail, and iron jaws.
> (*Yasht* 10, 70)

Mithra

Mithra is the best-known divinity of the Iranian pantheon, partly due to the spread and popularity of Mithraism in the Roman empire. The Avestan word *mithra* means 'pact, contract, covenant'. In *Yasht* 10, the *Mihr Yasht*, Mithra appears watching over men and their deeds, agreements and contracts. He is the guide towards the right order (*asha*) and is also responsible for giving protection against attack. As the god who controlled the cosmic order – that is, night and day and the change of seasons – he was associated with fire and the sun, and thus eventually became known as the sun god in both Iran and India. He is described as:

> [he] who first of the heavenly gods reaches over the Hara [Alburz Mountains], before the undying, swift-horsed sun; who, foremost in a golden array, takes hold of the beautiful summits, and ftom thence looks over the abode of the Aryans [Iranian peoples] with a beneficent eye.
> (*Yasht* 10, 13)

Among his many other qualities is his sense of justice: he protects the faithful and punishes the unfaithful. In this connection he is associated with warriors, and is described as riding on a chariot pulled by white horses. He carries a silver spear, wears a golden cuirass, and is further armed with golden-shafted arrows, axes, maces and daggers. Mithra is

> the lord of wide pastures, who is truth-speaking . . . with a thousand ears . . . with ten thousand eyes . . . strong, sleepless, and ever awake.
> (*Yasht* 10, 7)

The mace or club of Mithra is a powerful weapon not only against untruthful humans but also against the Evil Spirit, Angra Mainyu:

> . . . a club with a hundred knots, a hundred edges, that rushes forward and fells men down; a club cast out of red brass . . .; the strongest of all weapons, the most victorious of all weapons; from whom Angra Mainyu, who is all death, flees away in fear.
> (*Yasht* 10, 96-7)

To this day, new Zoroastrian priests receive the mace of Mithra to help them combat evil. The festival of Mithra, the *Mithrakana* (modern *Mihrigan*) was the celebration of the autumn equinox. The present month of *Mihr* (October) is named after the god Mithra.

One of Mithra's most important duties is to protect the Kingly Fortune or Divine Glory (*khvarnah* or *farr*). Only the legitimate rulers of the Iranians were privileged to possess the Divine Glory, which would abandon a king if he strayed from the righteous path (as will be seen in the case of King Yima). In protecting the *khvarnah*, Mithra is helped by Apam Napat, the god of water.

Perhaps best known to Westerners is the association of the 'Persian God' with the Roman cult of Mithras. The Persian origin of Mithraism is not disputed, but there may be no clear relationship with Zoroastrianism. Scenes depicting the bull-slaying Mithras are no longer seen as the fight of good against evil. Nor are they now interpreted as the killing of the first bull and the creation of the world through the purified seeds of the slaughtered animal. Instead the familiar reliefs decorating Mithraeums all over the Western world are interpreted within an astrological context.

Vayu

Vayu, the god of wind, is also depicted as a warrior god who chases the Evil Spirit with his sharp spear and golden weapons to protect the good creations of Ahura Mazda. He rules between the realms of Ahura Mazda and Angra Mainyu, between light and darkness.

Silver plate of the late 4th century AD, *with two investiture scenes in superimposed registers. The central figure holding a diadem (signifying king/divinity) is seated on a bench throne (takht) supported by two Simurgh-type creatures.*

Marble sculpture of the god Mithras slaying a bull. From Rome, probably 2nd century AD.

Tishtrya

Tishtrya, the god of rains, is personified as the star Sirius or Canis Major. His opponents are the witch Duzhyairya (Bad Harvest) and, worse still, Apaosha (Drought). He is vividly described as the god who rises from the source of all waters, the Vourukasha Sea, and who divides the waters among the countries. In his battle with Apaosha:

> . . . the bright and glorious Tishtrya goes down to the sea Vouru-Kasha in the shape of a white, beautiful horse, with golden ears and a golden caparison. But there rushes down to meet him the Daeva Apaosha, in the shape of a dark horse, black with black ears, black with a black back, black with a black tail, stamped with brands of terror. They meet together, hoof against hoof, O Spitama Zarathustra! the bright and glorious Tishtrya and the Daeva Apaosha.
> (*Yasht* 8, 20–2)

When the demon of drought starts to win, Tishtrya flees from the Vourukasha Sea and complains that if men had worshipped him in the proper fashion,

> [he] should have taken. . . the strength of ten horses, the strength of ten camels, the strength of ten bulls, the strength of ten mountains, the strength of ten rivers.
> (*Yasht* 8, 24)

When finally Zoroaster himself offers a sacrifice to Tishtrya, the god again descends as a white horse to the sea to meet his opponent. Once again they fight hoof against hoof, but this time

the bright and glorious Tishtrya proves stronger than the Daeva Apaosha, and he overcomes him.
(*Yasht* 8, 28)

The god of rains succeeds in making water pour down upon the fields, upon the whole world, and vapour rising from the sea moves forward in the form of clouds, pushed by the wind. The fourth month of the Iranian calendar is called *Tir* after the god Tishtrya, and the festival of *Tiragan* was celebrated as a rain festival.

Atar

Atar (Fire) in Zoroastrianism is regarded as the son of Ahura Mazda, the Wise Lord. Humans were expected to offer meat as a sacrifice to Atar, at the same time holding a bundle of sacred twigs (barsom) in the hand. Every house was expected to have a hearth for making sacrifices, in front of which prayers could be said:

. . . O Atar, son of Ahura Mazda! Thou art worthy of sacrifice and invocation; mayest thou receive the sacrifice and the invocation in the houses of men.
(*Atash Niyayesh* 7)

Atar is closely associated with the god Mithra: for example, together they succeed in rescuing the Divine Glory from the demon Azhi Dahaka. Atar is described as riding behind Mithra's chariot. Atar's part in the struggle with Azhi Dahaka over the Divine Glory in *Zamyad Yasht* is one of the few surviving myths about Atar:

. . . But Atar, the son of Ahura Mazda, advanced behind him, speaking in these words: 'There give it to me, thou three-mouthed Azhi Dahaka. If thou seizest that Glory that cannot be forcibly seized, then I will enter thy hinder part, I will blaze up in thy jaws, so that thou mayest never more rush upon the earth made by Mazda and destroy the world of the good principle.' Then Azhi took back his hands, as the instinct of life prevailed, so much had Atar affrighted him.
(*Yasht* 19, 49–51)

Reverse of a coin of the first Sasanian king, Ardashir I (c. AD224–42). The fire altar is symbolic of Zoroastrianism, which became the official religion of the Sasanian state.

To this day, fire has continued to play a prominent part in Zoroastrian religion and is still worshipped in fire-temples. Fire is a symbol of Zoroastrianism. In Sasanian times the three famous eternal fires, each representing one of the three classes of society, were the Farnabag fire (priests), the Gushnasp fire (warriors) and the Burzin Mihr fire (workers). The Gushnasp fire was probably burning at Takht-i Sulaiman in north-western Iran. To this day the Bahram fire, the most sacred of all fires, is necessary to fight the forces of darkness and evil and is regarded as the symbol of truth.

Haoma

Haoma (Vedic Soma) is the god who gives health and strength, and who provides rich harvests and sons. His name is that of a plant with healing potency, believed to be of the genus *Ephedra*. The juice of the plant gave supernatural powers and had an intoxicating effect. The god was thought to give strength to overcome any enemy. Indeed, when Kavi Haosravah (later Kay Khusrow) defeated the Turanian king Franrasyan (Afrasiyab), he had the physical assistance of Haoma.

The creation of the world

The ancient Iranians, believed that the sky was the first part of the world to be created. It was originally described as a round empty shell made of rock crystal, passing beneath as well as above the earth. Later it was thought to be made of metal. Next to be created was water, followed by the earth. Then came plants and animals. Human beings were the sixth creation, and fire probably the seventh and last.

Mountains were believed to have grown from the surface of the earth, originally a flat disc that encompassed the Western as well as the Eastern world.

View of the peak of Mount Demavand in the Alburz Mountains, north of Tehran.

Certain place names have been linked with the creation of the world. For example, Alburz (Mount Hara or Harburz) is described in the *Avesta* (*Yasht* 19, 1) as the first mountain in the world, which took 800 years to grow, its roots reaching deep into the ground and its peak attached to the sky. It is the most important mountain. The Iranians, like the Indians, believed that the world was divided into seven regions or *karshvar* (*keshvar* in modern Persian, which means country). These regions were created when rain first fell upon the earth. The central region, the Khvanirath, inhabited by humans, was as large as the other six put together. The *Bundahishn* describes it as follows:

> On the nature of the earth, it says in revelation, that there are thirty and three kinds of land. On the day when Tistar [god of rain] produced the rain, when its seas arose therefrom, the whole place, half taken up by water, was converted into seven portions; this portion, as much as one-half, is the middle and six portions are around; those six portions are together as much as *Khvaniras*. The name *keshvar* is also applied to them and they existed side by side . . . And of these seven regions every benefit was created in Khvaniras . . . For the Kayanians and heroes were created in Khvaniras; and the good religion of the Mazdayasnians was created in Khvaniras, and afterwards conveyed to the other regions.
> (XI, 1-6)

It is in Khvaniras (Khvanirath) that the Peak of Hara (Alburz) was believed to have grown from the roots of the Alburz Mountains; the stars, moon and sun were thought to move around this peak. Alburz is described thus in the *Bundahishn*:

> On the nature of mountains, it says in revelation, that, at first, the mountains have grown forth in eighteen years; and Alburz ever grew till the completion of eight hundred years; two hundred years up to the star station, two hundred years to the moon station, two hundred years to the sun station, and two hundred years to the endless light. The other mountains have grown out of Alburz, in number 2244 . . .
> (XII, 1-2)

While Alburz or Mount Hara was the source for both light and water, the Vourukasha Sea is described in the *Avesta* as the gathering point of water. This important sea occupied 'one third of the earth, to the south, on the skirts of the Harburz' (*Vendidad* 21, 16), and was fed by a huge river, the Harahvaiti. Two great rivers flowed out from the sea to the east and the west, thus forming the boundaries of the inhabited world. The rivers were cleansed as they passed around the earth and, when they returned to the Vourukasha, their clean water was taken back up to the Peak of Hara.

In the middle of the Vourukasha grew the mother of all trees, the source of all plants, described in the *Avesta* (*Yasht* 12, 17) as the Saena Tree, Tree of All Remedies or Tree of All Seeds. This first tree held the nest of Saena (Senmurv in Pahlavi, Simurgh in Persian), the legendary bird. It also produced the seeds of all plants. Another important plant growing nearby was the 'mighty Gaokerena', which had healing properties when eaten and gave immortality to the resurrected bodies of the dead.

The first animal in the world was the 'uniquely created bull', white in colour and as bright as the moon. According to Zoroastrian tradition it was

A moulded stucco plaque from Chal Tarkhan, Ray, showing the mythical bird Senmurv (Simurgh). Late Sasanian, 7th–8th century AD.

killed by Angra Mainyu, the Evil Spirit, and its seed was carried up to the moon. Once thoroughly purified, this seed produced many species of animals. It also sprouted into plants when part of it fell to the ground.

The home of the uniquely created bull was on the bank of the River Veh Daiti (Veh Rod), which flowed to the east from the Vourukasha Sea. On the opposite bank lived Gayomartan (Gayomard in Pahlavi, Kiyumars in the *Shahnameh*). In *Yasht* 13, 87 he is described as the first man, as wide as he was tall and as 'bright as the sun'. Gayomartan was slain by Angra Mainyu, but the sun purified his seed and, after forty years, a rhubarb plant sprang from it. This slowly grew into Mashya and Mashyanag, the first mortal man and woman. Beguiled by Angra Mainyu, they turned to him as the creator and thus committed the first sin. Instead of peace and harmony, their world was filled with corruption and evil. Only after fifty years were they able to produce offspring, but the first twins were eaten by their parents. After a long period of childlessness another set of twins was finally born, and from these sprang not only the human race but specifically the Iranian peoples.

On the nature of men, it says in revelation that Gayomard, in passing away, gave forth seed; that seed was thoroughly purified by the motion of the light of the sun . . . and in forty years, with the shape of a one-stemmed Rivas-plant [rhubarb J, and the fifteen years of its fifteen leaves, Matro and Matroyao [Mashya and MashyanagJ grew up from the earth in such a manner that their arms rested behind on their shoulders, and one joined to the other they were connected together and both alike . . . And both of them changed from the shape of a plant into the shape of man, and the breath went spiritually into them, which is the soul; . . . Ahura Mazda spoke: . . . 'You are man, you are the ancestry of the world, and you are created in perfect devotion by me; perform devotedly the duty of the law . . . speak good words, do good deeds, and worship no demons . . .' And afterwards antagonism rushed into their minds, and their minds were thoroughly corrupted, and they exclaimed that the Evil Spirit created the water and earth, plants and animals.
(*Bundahishn* xv, 1–9)

Demons, fabulous creatures and heroes

The *Avesta* and other religious texts of the Zoroastrian faith describe demons, fabulous creatures and human heroes who inhabited the world of the ancient Iranians. The most informative source is the *Avesta*, but later texts such as the *Bundahishn* also tell at great length of the ancient heroes and their opponents.

Demons and evil powers

Two types of evil power were common in the early Iranian world: those which attacked the bodies of humans directly and those which moved around them, waiting for an opportunity to harm them and their crops and animals.

Evil beings in general were known as *yatu*, but the word was also used for their opposites: those who were able to combat evil and its power. These were the sorcerers and magicians. (The modern Persian word for magic and sorcery is *jadu*, and *jadugar* is a magician, sorcerer.) The demons were called *div*, a term which had its origin in the ancient word *daeva*, meaning god or false god (cf. Latin *deus*). There was also a group of female evils called *pairaka* (modern Persian *pari*; cf. English fairy) who were most active during the night and had a witch-like personality. *Pairaka* appeared in different guises: for example, they could take the form of a rat or a shooting star. Sometimes they made themselves beautiful in order to seduce and harm men, and in later Persian tradition their beauty is often praised. The most evil demon was the female spirit Naush, who in later Zoroastrian tradition appears as a mottled fly from the north – the source and homeland of all evil. She belongs to the group of evil beings described as *drug* (in modern Persian, *durugh* means lie). One of the opponents of the *divs* and *pairaka* was the god Mithra.

Fabulous creatures

Among the fabulous creatures mentioned in Zoroastrian texts, the legendary bird Saena (Pahlavi Senmurv), a great falcon, enjoys a particular prominence. She sits on top of the Tree of All Seeds, and by beating her wings causes the seeds to scatter. These are then carried away by rain and wind and distributed over the earth. According to later legends she suckles young ones, and although her

Silver gilt plate with a Senmurv, 'the king of birds'. The Senmurv (Simurgh) is a combination of bird and dog or lion. Late Sasanian, 7th–8th century AD.

identification with the later Simurgh is probable but not certain, it is interesting to see how in Firdowsi's *Shahnameh* a similar legendary bird with supernatural powers plays a prominent role in the story of Zal and his son Rustam.

The Tree of All Seeds stands in the middle of the Vourukasha Sea and is protected by a fish, the Kara, which swims around it and is able to keep all harmful creatures away. Particularly dangerous is the frog which tries to gnaw at the sacred tree's roots. Another fabulous creature whose task is to protect the tree is the righteous ass. This white-bodied creature has a golden horn on its head, three legs, six eyes and nine mouths. It too stands in the middle of the Vourukasha Sea and destroys all the harmful beings in the water.

Apart from Saena, other birds mentioned in the *Avesta* are Karshiptar, the 'swiftly flying', which is supposed to have spread the prophet Zoroaster's words, and Ashozushta, the owl, which scares off evil demons by muttering holy words. Then there is the bird Chamrush, whose patriotic task is to peck non-Iranians and who helps to distribute the seeds from the Tree of All Seeds.

Silver gilt plate depicting a king on horseback hunting lions. Sasanian, 5th century AD. *Lions were still present in south-western Iran at the beginning of the 20th century.*

The harmful creatures, like demons, were felt to be a constant threat to mankind, animals, plants and crops. Known as *khrafstra*, they include beasts of prey, rodents, frogs, lizards, tortoises, spiders and insects such as wasps, ants and beetles. Cats were disliked because they were regarded as belonging to the same family as dangerous tigers and lions. Among these unpopular creatures were also the fabulous monsters which were challenged by human heroes. They usually took the form of serpents or dragons (*azhi*). The most important of these was the Azhi Dahaka (modern Persian *azhdaha*), the monster with three heads who ate humans. The same three-headed, man-devouring monster appears as Zahhak in Firdowsi's *Shahnameh*. In the *Avesta*, the Azhi Dahaka is described as:

> . . . the three-mouthed, the three-headed, the six-eyed, who has a thousand senses, that most powerful, fiendish *Drug*, that demon, baleful to the world, the strongest *Drug* that Angra Mainyu created against the material world, to destroy the world of the good principle.
> (*Yasht* 9, 14)

In another section of the *Avesta*, the *Aban Yasht*, the Azhi Dahaka beseeches Ardvi Sura Anahita, the goddess of water, for assistance in his attempt to seize the Divine Glory:

> To her did Azhi Dahaka, the three-mouthed, offer up a sacrifice in the land of Bawri [Babylon?], with a hundred male horses, a thousand oxen, and ten thousand lambs. He begged of her a boon, saying: 'Grant me this boon, O good most beneficent Ardvi Sura Anahita! that I may make all the seven Karshvares [countries] of the earth empty of men.'
> (*Yasht* 5, 29–30)

This is after the Divine Glory has abandoned the sinful King Yima, two of whose daughters were married to the Azhi Dahaka. This monster is unable to succeed against Atar, the god of fire, who saves the Glory by taking it to the Vourukasha Sea. He is finally defeated by Thraetaona (Fariydun of the *Shahnameh*), who keeps him captive until the end of the world. At this time he will escape only to be slain by Keresaspa (also known as Garshasp).

Other dragons or *azhis* are the horned, yellow-green Azhi Sruvara, which devours horses and men; the golden-heeled Gandareva which terrorises the Vourukasha Sea; and young Snavidhka, which intends to use the spirits of good and evil to pull his chariot when he is fully grown up. There is also a huge evil bird, Kamak; he and the other harmful fabulous creatures are the enemies of mankind, but they themselves fall victim to the heroes. Here is the triumph of good over evil, a struggle central to the Zoroastrian religion.

The first man and heroes

Some of the legendary heroes described in the *Avesta* and later Zoroastrian holy texts probably belong to the pre-Zoroastrian period. At this earlier stage the Indian-speaking and Iranian-speaking peoples, who were related through their language, had not yet separated. With the advent of the prophet Zoroaster and the spread of Zoroastrianism in Iran, some of the ancient pre-Zoroastrian concepts and traditions were incorporated into the *Avesta*, particularly in that part of it known as the *Yasht*. The *Zamyad Yasht* (that is, *Yasht* 19) gives a detailed description of these early heroes, almost all of whom reappear in Firdowsi's *Shahnameh*, written more than two thousand years later. This part of the *Yasht* provides an early short version of the *Shahnameh*.

Gayomartan, whose name means 'Mortal Life', is the mythical first man. Described as 'bright as the sun', he is a large and impressive figure who was created out of earth:

> We worship the Fravashi [the deified souls] of Gaya Maretan, who first listened unto the thought and teaching of Ahura Mazda; of whom Ahura formed the face of the Aryan [Iranian] nations, the seed of the Aryan nations.
> (*Yasht* 13, 87)

Gayomartan falls victim to the Evil Spirit, but his seed is purified by the sun after his death. Forty years after being returned to the earth, his seed becomes a rhubarb plant from which the first mortal man and woman develop.

Illustration from an 18th-century Kashmiri abridged prose Shahnameh, showing the early mythical king Hushang.

The mythological kings of the Iranians begin with the Paradata dynasty (Pishdadian of the *Shahnameh*) and their first king, Haoshanha (Hushang of the *Shahnameh*). In the *Aban Yasht* he appears as Haoshanha, the Paradata, who asks the goddess of water, Ardvi Sura Anahita, for help to overcome the demons and other evil powers.

He is succeeded by Takhma Urupi (Tahmuras of the *Shahnameh*) who ruled over the seven countries, over the evil beings and demons, and who 'rode Angra Mainyu, turned into the shape of horse, all around the earth from one end to the other, for thirty years' (*Yasht* 19, 28-9).

The greatest hero of Iranian mythology was undoubtedly Yima (Jamshid of the *Shahnameh*). As Yima Khshaeta, King Yima, he belongs to the Indo-Iranian traditions. The Indian equivalent, the Vedic Yama, chooses to die and becomes the king of the dead. The Avestan Yima is 'the fair Yima', 'the good shepherd' (*Vendidad* 11, 21). He is highly regarded in the mythical land of Airyaneum Vaejah (Eranvej in Pahlavi), the centre of the world for the ancient Iranians and probably their traditional homeland (that is, Khorezmia). He is described as the king whose rule extended over the entire world; a world where everything was good. He says:

> I will nourish, and rule, and watch over thy world. There shall be, while I am king, neither cold wind nor hot wind, neither disease nor death.
> (*Vendidad* 11, 5)

After three hundred years of his rule, when the world has become over-full of men, animals and birds, Yima enlarges it by one third with his golden stick and whip. Twice more, after six hundred and nine hundred years respectively, he again enlarges the world. Then Yima sins by telling a lie, and the Divine Glory abandons him:

But when he began to find delight in words of falsehood and untruth, the Glory was seen to flee away from him in the shape of a bird. When his Glory had disappeared, then the great Yima Khshaeta, the good shepherd, trembled and was in sorrow before his foes; he was confounded and laid him down on the ground.
(*Yasht* 19, 34)

Yima appears once again as the King of Paradise in connection with the birth of the prophet Zoroaster. The description of him in the *Vendidad,* the part of the *Avesta* which probably dates to the second and early third centuries AD, is particularly interesting. Here, a different picture is painted of his character, with no reference to his sin, and he takes part in an epic resembling the Mesopotamian story of the flood. In this version, Yima rules for a thousand years, after which the gods announce that bad times of frost and cold lie ahead and that he should look after one man and woman and specimens of the best animals and plants. Later Zoroastrian legends make Yima immortal, but in Persian folklore and the epic *Shahnameh,* he sins and dies.

Thraetaona is best remembered for his fight with Azhi Dahaka, whom he does not kill but keeps captive in Mount Demavand until the end of the world (*Bundahishn* XXIX, 9). In the *Avesta* his genealogy is also mentioned:

Then Thraetaona seized that Glory, he, the heir of the valiant Athwya clan, who was the most victorious of all victorious men next to Zarathustra; who smote Azhi Dahaka . . .
(*Yasht* 19, 36-7)

Before his encounter with the dragon, Thraetaona asks the water goddess Ardvi Sura Anahita for help and offers her a sacrifice of 'a hundred male horses, a thousand oxen, ten thousand lambs' (*Yasht* 5, 33). He then mentions the two beautiful wives of the Azhi Dahaka, Savanghavak and Erenavak (Shahrnaz and Arnavaz in the *Shahnameh*). In *Farvardin Yasht* (*Yasht* 13, 131), Thraetaona also has the ability to cure certain illnesses and can help 'against itch, hot fever, humours, cold fever, and incontinence' and 'against the evil done by the serpent'. Thraetaona was therefore esteemed as both warrior and physician.

Keresaspa (Garshasp) appears in the *Avesta* as a member of the family of Sam. In the *Shahnameh*, Sam is the grandfather of Rustam, but there does not seem to be a link between the hero of the *Avesta* and Sam of the *Shahnameh*. Keresaspa is described (*Yasht* 13, 136) as curly-haired, very strong, and possessing a club or mace:

Then the manly-hearted Keresaspa seized that Glory; he who was the sturdiest of men of strength, next to Zarathustra, for his manly courage.
(*Yasht* 19, 38)

As well as fighting against evil forces, he also engages in battles with dragons, the most famous of these being his encounter with and killing of the horned

Silver bowl showing a figure, probably a king, reclining at a banquet. He has a bushy tripartite hairstyle and wears an elaborate outfit. Parthian, late 2nd–early 3rd century AD.

Sruvara. But once, when Keresaspa is cooking his meal over a fire outside, he does not realise that the dragon is sleeping below the vegetation over which the fire has been made. The monster is woken by the heat, and in moving to run away, causes the pot to fall into the fire. The pollution of the fire is a sin, so Keresaspa is not allowed to enter paradise after his death until Zoroaster himself pleads on the hero's behalf.

The dynasty of the mythical Paradata was succeeded by the Kavi kings of Iran (Kiyanian of the *Shahnameh*) who included Kavi Vishtaspa, the patron of Zoroaster, Kavi Usan, and Kavi Haosravah (Kay Gushtasp, Kay Kavus and Kay Khusrow of the *Shahnameh*). These kings are greatly honoured in the

Avesta, expressed by their possession of the Divine Glory (*khvarnah*). However, also in quest of the Divine Glory is their main opponent, Franrasyan from Turya, the land to the north and east of Iran, which in the *Avesta* counts as one of the five divisions of the Iranians. The name Turya, according to later legends, derives from Tur, son of Thraetaona. According to the *Shahnameh*, King Thraetaona (Fariydun) divided his kingdom between his three sons, Iraj, Salm and Tur. These three appear in the *Bundahishn* (XXXI, 9) as 'Salm, Tug and Airik, the sons of Fredun'. Iraj received the main part (that is, Iran), while Salm was given the western part and Tur the eastern part. It was only after the arrival of Turkish tribes in the areas to the east of the Caspian Sea that a misunderstanding occurred and the ancient Turya of the *Avesta* and its ruler Franrasyan were identified as Turks. In fact, Iranian-speaking peoples occupied Central Asia well before the sixth century AD. *Zamyad Yasht* contains a detailed account of Franrasyan's struggle to obtain the Divine Glory from the Iranian rulers:

> He stripped himself naked, wishing to seize that Glory that belongs to the Aryan nations, born and unborn, and to the holy Zarathustra . . . Then the most crafty Turanian Franrasyan rushed down into the sea Vouru-Kasha, O Spitama Zarathustra . . .
> (*Yasht* 19, 56, 58)

Franrasyan is not only the opponent of the Kavis, the Iranian kings, but also a general symbol of evil. He continually attempts to overthrow the Iranian kings in order to obtain their Divine Glory. His evil makes him comparable to a demon:

> The Turanian ruffian Franrasyan tried to seize to rule over all the Karshvares [countries]; round about the seven Karshvares did that ruffian Franrasyan rush, trying to seize the Glory of Zarathustra. But that Glory escaped to hidden inlets of the sea.
> (*Yasht* 19, 82)

He is finally defeated by Kavi Haosravah, who avenges the brutal murder of his father Siyavarshan (Siyavush of the *Shahnameh*). A large part of the *Shahnameh* is devoted to Prince Siyavush, including his marriage to Afrasiyab's daughter Farangis, and his murder by Afrasiyab and his brother Garsivaz (Keresavazda of the *Avesta*):

> To her [Drvaspa, the deity who cares for cattle] did the gallant Husravah, he who united the Aryan nations into one kingdom, offer up a sacrifice, behind the Kaekasta lake, the deep lake of salt waters, with a hundred male horses, a thousand oxen, ten thousand lambs, and an offering of libations: 'Grant me this boon, O good, most beneficent Drvaspa! that I may kill the Turanian murderer, Franrasyan, behind the Kaekasta lake, the deep lake of salt waters, to avenge the murder of my father Syavarshana . . .'
> (*Yasht* 19, 21–2)

The Book of Kings: Firdowsi's Shahnameh

Written in some 50,000 couplets or double-verses by the poet Firdowsi, the *Shahnameh* or *Book of Kings* is an epic that describes the myths, legends and history of Iran's pre-Islamic past. Firdowsi, who was born in Tus (Khurasan) to a family of landowners (*dihqan*), completed his *Shahnameh* around AD 1010, some three and a half centuries after the Arab conquest of Iran. The *Shahnameh*, which was dedicated to Sultan Mahmud, the Ghaznavid ruler, is regarded not only as a work of great literary importance, but also as a valuable source of information on the traditions, customs and folklore of pre-Islamic Iran.

What were Firdowsi's sources? The poet himself writes that, apart from oral traditions, he had access to written records. Among these are some thousand verses by the poet Daqiqi, who was murdered at the end of the tenth century before he could finish his version of the *Book of Kings*:

> Although he only rhymed the veriest mite
> One thousand couplet full of feast and fight
> He was my pioneer and he alone
> In that he set the Shāhs upon the throne . . .
> To sing the praises of the kings was his
> And crown the princes with his eulogies
> (V, V. 1555)

Many other sources were available to Firdowsi as well, and he is most particular in indicating whether the stories came from a written source or whether they were passed on to him by oral tradition. In the late Sasanian period, the sixth and seventh centuries AD, the mythological past and early history of Iran had been recorded in the official *Khvadaynamak* (*Khudaynameh*), an epic written in Pahlavi (Middle Persian) which no longer exists. This and other Pahlavi books were translated into Arabic in the eighth century, and translations into Persian soon followed. In addition to the Persian translation of the *Khudaynameh* and other Pahlavi sources, Firdowsi's other important written record was the prose *Shahnameh* of Abu Mansur, known as *Shahnameh-yi Abu Mansuri*, of the mid tenth century AD. Unfortunately this *Shahnameh* no longer exists, but Firdowsi's epic is a poetic version of it. His achievement – that of reviving and securing the Persian language as well as Iran's mythological past and early history – thus builds on a long oral and written tradition.

Early 19th century painting of Kiyumars, the first man and ruler, who dressed in a leopard skin and lived in a cave. Apart from his spotted trousers (indicating the leopard skin), the rest of his outfit and jewelled sword are typical of the Qajar period.

The early myths of the *Shahnameh*

The actual epic of the *Shahnameh* begins with the dynasty of the Pishdadian (the Paradates of the *Avesta*). The first mythological figure described is Kiyumars (the first man, Gayomartan or Gayomard of the *Avesta*). Here he is the ruler who introduces the throne and the crown, the master of the world. He lives in the mountains, ruling over mankind and all creatures, wild and tame. Dressed in a leopard skin which signifies courage and manhood, Kiyumars symbolises the early period in human evolution, a cave dweller who becomes the highest ruler through courage. It is at his court that religion is introduced to people who come from far and wide in search of spiritual and religious values. Kiyumars is the perfect ruler, possessor of all the necessary symbols of kingship – that is, the throne, the crown and the castle. But this perfect harmony comes to an abrupt end when tragedy strikes. As in many of Firdowsi's stories, the tragic event is the death of a beloved son – in this particular story, one who is killed by a *div*, a black demon.

The *Shahnameh* then relates that another mythological ruler, Hushang (Haoshanha of the *Avesta*), the grandson of Kiyumars and son of Siyamak, 'the king of seven countries', was involved in the development of civilisation in the world. His achievements include the discovery of fire, the separation of iron from rock, the smith's craft, tools and weapons, and the irrigation and cultivation of land with the sowing of seeds. In other words, the invention of many important techniques and skills is attributed to this early period. Tahmuras (Takhma Urupi of the *Avesta*), Hushang's son, is described as the one who successfully confronts the demons and, by

Illustration from an 18th-century Kashmiri abridged prose Shahnameh showing Tahmuras, the conqueror of demons, receiving two humble divs, who beseech the king not to kill them.

capturing Ahriman (Angra Mainyu) through magic, rides around the earth on the back of the evil being (there is a parallel story in the *Avesta*). The *divs* beg for mercy and promise to teach Tahmuras the skills of reading and writing.

> The captives bound and stricken begged their lives.
> 'Destroy us not', they said, 'and we will teach thee
> A new and fruitful art' . . .
> (I, v. 22)

The reign of Jamshid

The reign of Jamshid (Yima of the *Avesta*) was an age of invention, partly as a result of the need for more sophisticated weapons of war. In order to protect the ruler and the realm from enemies, a class of warriors is created, marking the beginning of a rigid class structure at an early date in human social development. The epic reveals that there is also a caste of priests, as well as peasants, farmers and artisans. Each of the different groups was kept busy with a specially designed task, and even the so-called unclean demons were given the job of mixing earth with water to make bricks. Using stone and gypsum, they built baths and monumental palaces.

With Jamshid, perhaps the most famous king of Persian mythology, a new and important royal symbol is introduced in the *Shahnameh*: the Divine Glory (*farr-i izadi*) that gave him his famous throne, on which he sat like the shining sun. To celebrate this event, the festival of *Now Ruz*, the new day or the first day of the New Year, was introduced. On this day the world gathered around the king's throne, paid homage to him and celebrated with wine, music and dance. Modern Iranians, as well as Parsees (Zoroastrians in India) and some nations of Central Asia, celebrate this same festival on 21 March, the spring equinox. In Iran, celebrations last up to thirteen days in honour of the beginning of the season of growth. The festival of *Chahar Shanbeh Suri*, which marks the end of winter, is on the eve of the last Wednesday before *Now Ruz*. People gather dried twigs, desert bushes or brush wood, place them in seven bundles in the yard or street, and set them alight at sunset. Then they jump over the fire. Also common at this time and during the *Now Ruz* celebrations is the burning of rice seeds (*isfand*) or frankincense (*kondor*) against the evil eye and all bad spirits.

The three hundred years of peace and harmony of Jamshid's reign are disrupted through human greed, as so often happens in the *Shahnameh*. Jamshid ceases to believe in a higher power and regards himself as the only and ultimate ruler. His proclamation to this effect upsets the priests and he soon loses his Divine Glory. His army abandons him and the world is thrown into confusion. The way is then open for evil to strike in the form of Ahriman, who gains supremacy over mankind and ushers in a long period of injustice. It is during this era of darkness that Ahriman appears disguised as Zahhak (Azhi Dahaka in the *Avesta*), who through ignorance and greed has sold his soul to the devil.

Zahhak, the serpent-shouldered ruler

It is interesting that Zahhak, who falls into a trap laid by the devil, is described in the *Shahnameh* as the son of a respectable and honest man from the Arabian plains. Because of his association with Mesopotamia in later Zoroastrian texts such as the *Bundahishn*, it is thought that Zahhak's identification as an Arab stems from the Iranians' dislike of the Arab conquest and control of their country. Firdowsi first describes Zahhak as a true hero, a *pahlavan*, brave as his father, who spends most of his time on horseback. But youthful innocence leads him into the arms of the devil, who exploits his unawareness of evil. By disguising himself as a visitor, the devil uses his persuasiveness and charm to capture Zahhak's devotion, finally succeeding in getting the young man to swear allegiance to him. As a result, Zahhak finally agrees, with great reluctance, to murder his father.

It is fascinating to see how this unlawful and evil pact with the devil is marked by a change in Zahhak's appearance. When his benefactor embraces him, two black snakes suddenly grow out of his shoulders. Not only is it impossible for Zahhak to remove the ugly monsters, but he also has to feed them

Illustration from an 18th-century Kashmiri abridged prose Shahnameh showing the enthroned 'snake-shouldered Zahhak' witnessing the execution of King Jamshid.

with the brains of humans every day. Zahhak tries desperately to kill the snakes by cutting their heads off, but they simply grow new heads.

> A marvel followed – from the monarch's shoulders
> Grew two black snakes. Distraught he sought a cure
> And in the end excised them, but they grew
> Again! Oh strange! like branches from a tree . . .
> . . . At length Iblis [the devil] himself came hurrying
> Tight as a leech. 'This was thy destiny',
> He said, 'cut not the snakes, but let them live.
> Give them men's brains and gorge them till they sleep.'
> (I, V. 32, 33)

Meanwhile Jamshid, whose god-like pretensions have caused him to lose royal power, crown and throne, drives his men into the arms of Zahhak and the devil when they go in search of a new ruler. Zahhak, though an Arab, is hailed as the new king of Iran, after which he marries Jamshid's two daughters, Shahrnaz and Arnavaz (Savanghavak and Erenavak in the *Avesta*). His rule lasts for a thousand years, during which time darkness reigns over the country as young men are sacrificed daily to the serpents rising from his shoulders.

> Zahhak sat on the throne a thousand years
> Obeyed by all the world. Through that long time
> The customs of the wise were out of vogue . . .
> All virtue was despised, black art esteemed,
> Right lost to night, disaster manifest.
> (I, V. 35)

Gradually discontent grows among the population until a group of noblemen plot a revolt, with the aim of offering the crown of Iran to a royal prince of the house of Jamshid. The leader of the noblemen is Kaveh, a blacksmith, who has lost eighteen sons to Zahhak.

The triumph of good over evil

Like many other characters in the *Shahnameh,* Zahhak foresees his own death in a dream, in which a royal offspring appears as tall as a cypress tree, carrying a mace resembling a bull's head. This youth captures him, ties him up and throws him into a well. Zahhak is told by one of his priests that the dream will indeed come true, and that a hero called Fariydun (Thraetaona of the *Avesta*), reaching the moon in height, would look for the royal insignia of belt, crown, throne and tiara. Fariydun's birth is then described in great detail by Firdowsi who, by relating how the baby was fed by a cow, emphasises its physical strength. Fear of being found by Zahhak prompts Fariydun's mother to flee to the Alburz Mountains and take refuge there with her young child. When the day comes for Kaveh to organise the uprising against Zahhak, he leads his followers to Fariydun's hiding-place in the mountains. Wrapped around a spear Kaveh carries the royal banner, the *darafsh-i kaviani,* a piece of leather which the blacksmith had originally worn over his legs. The *Shahnameh* relates that, ever

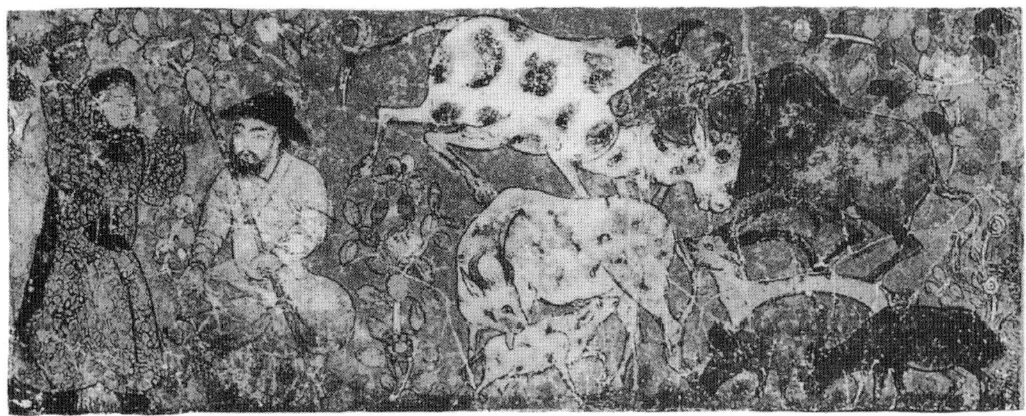

Illustration from a 14th-century Shahnameh showing Fariydun, son of Abtin, carried on his mother's shoulders to the Alburz Mountains, where he is entrusted to a cowherd for protection from the wicked Zahhuk.

since that day, the banner had to be covered with jewels each time a new king was chosen.

> . . . Thenceforth when any Shāh
> Ascended to the throne, and donned the crown,
> He hung the worthless apron of the smith
> With still more jewels, sumptuous brocade,
> And painted silk of Chin [China] . . .
> (I, v. 48)

Before setting off on his campaign, Fariydun orders that a mace be fashioned for him by the blacksmith, which resembles a bull's head. The army, with him at its head and with Kaveh carrying the royal banner, marches towards

Illustration from an 18th-century Kashmiri abridged prose Shahnameh. Fariydun lifts his bull-headed mace and hits Zahhak on the head.

Mesopotamia where they have to cross *Arvand Rud* (the River Tigris). The final encounter between good and evil ends in victory for Fariydun, who, on the advice of an angel, takes the trussed-up devil to the mountains and leaves him there with blood pouring out of his heart. Fariydun's long rule of five hundred years marks an era of prosperity, harmony and peace in his realm and among his people.

The division of Fariydun's empire and its consequences

Once again, however, as often happens in the *Shahnameh*, good encounters evil when Fariydun divides his kingdom among his three sons and jealousy breaks out between them. Two of the brothers, Salm and Tur, were born to Jamshid's daughter Shahrnaz, while Iraj is the son of her sister Arnavaz. Fariydun gives his eldest son, Salm, the western part of the kingdom and his second son, Tur, is given Central Asia (Turan). But the most important part, Iran, and Fariydun's golden throne, go to Iraj, their half-brother. Although the youngest, he has proved to be the wisest and bravest of the three.

Soon Salm's discontent and anger over the division become uncontrollable and, together with Tur, he kills Iraj. The murder of one brother by the other two marks the triumph of evil and the beginning of an important episode in Persian mythology: the long and continuous encounters between the kingdoms of Iran and Turan (Airya and Turya of the *Avesta*) and the start of the heroic section of the *Book of Kings*, ushered in by the rule of King Manuchihr (Manushchithra of the *Avesta*), the grandson of Iraj. From this point on, the numerous battles described in the *Shahnameh* result from animosity and rivalry between the two kingdoms, both sides producing a number of famous heroes, but with the Iranians successfully withstanding the attacks and plots of the Turanians and their king, Afrasiyab (Franrasyan of the *Avesta*). The greatest hero of all time, Rustam, spends his life fighting the king of Turan and protecting the boundaries of Iran, as had his father, Zal, and his grandfather, Sam. Zal accompanies Manuchihr on his campaign to Tur to avenge his grandfather's murder. Firdowsi gives a detailed picture of the burial rites and mourning upon the death of Fariydun, describing how the corpse of the late king was placed inside a tomb along with red-coloured gold and lapis lazuli. An ivory throne was put under the body and a crown attached to it, and then the entrance of the tomb was sealed. After this, Manuchihr succeeds his great-grandfather Fariydun, and wears the royal tiara, *kolah*, on his head.

The family of Rustam

Rustam, the son of Zal and grandson of Sam, steps into the limelight at a time when Iran and Turan are continuously in conflict for the supremacy of land and crown. All the heroes on the Iranian side are described as brave, virtuous and deeply attached to the king of kings, for whom they are willing to risk their lives and sacrifice their dearest ones. This is particularly true of Rustam, as shown in the legend of his son Sohrab. Although the name of Rustam's grandfather, Sam, and that of his father Nariman appear in connection with the legendary Keresaspa (Garshasp) in later Zoroastrian texts, neither Rustam nor his son Sohrab is mentioned in the *Avesta*. It seems that the original legends of Rustam did not belong to the same group of stories that were incorporated in the *Avesta*, but were part of an independent cycle. Rustam and his family are described in the *Shahnameh* as kings of Sistan in eastern Iran, and often Rustam is described as Sagzi (Saka). Some scholars believe that Rustam dates from the Parthian period and the time in the first century AD when the Indo-Scythian kings formed an independent kingdom in eastern Iran. Whatever his historical position and origins may have been, Rustam became one of the greatest heroes of Persian mythology, a symbol of great physical strength, spiritual goodness and devotion to his country

Rustam's father, Zal, is described in detail in the *Shahnameh*, and his birth and upbringing are linked with the legendary guardian bird, the Simurgh (this powerful bird also plays an important part in Rustam's life, coming to his rescue more than once in times of crisis). When Zal is born, to parents who had long awaited a child, his father's joy changes to sorrow and utter helplessness when he sees the newborn baby. The boy's body is described as clean as silver and his face like paradise, but with hair as white as an old man's. Sam is so distressed to see his offspring with such an unusual feature that he becomes disillusioned with the world. In a passionate monologue with God, he questions the reason for his punishment in being given 'the son of Ahriman [the Devil] [with] his black eyes and hair like jasmine [in colour]. When heroes come and ask about this ill-omened child, I shall have to leave Iran with shame. What shall I say, that this is the child of a demon, a two-coloured leopard, or a supernatural being resembling a fairy?'

Sam finally abandons his child in the Alburz Mountains, which are 'near the sun and far from humans', leaving there 'the innocent offspring of a hero, who did not even know the difference between black and white'. But, as so often happens in mythological stories, the little baby survives with the intervention of God the Almighty, who causes Simurgh to discover him while she is flying over her kingdom of the Alburz to look for food for her brood. She takes the abandoned baby to feed to her young ones, but a voice tells her 'to look after this unweaned child, as a man would grow out of this seed'. Thus Zal grows up with Simurgh and her family. Meanwhile, news of a young cypress-like youth living in the mountains has spread to Sam's court, and when Sam tells his wise men about his dream, in which a horseman delivers a happy message about his son being alive, they urge him to go and find his son with the white hair and light-skinned body.

High up in the mountains Sam pleads with God to forgive him and to return his abandoned child, whom he acknowledges is 'not from the sperm of the ill-descended Ahriman'. Simurgh, watching from above, knows immediately why Sam has come to the mountains. She urges Zal to return to his father as her nest is no longer suitable for the son of the greatest of all heroes, the son

Illustration from an 18th-century Kashmiri abridged prose Shahnameh. The mythical bird Simurgh carries the newly born Zal to her nest in the Alburz Mountains. Simurgh's children are shown waiting for her return.

who one day will take over as king. But before returning the sad young hero to his father, Simurgh gives him one of her feathers to light as a signal at times of danger or trouble, and she promises him that she will appear at once.

> . . . Henceforth if men
> Shall hurt or, right or wrong, exclaim against thee,
> Then burn the feather and behold my might,
> For I have cherished thee beneath my plumes
> And brought thee up among my little ones.
> (I, V. 139)

Zal returns to the kingdom of his father in Zabulistan (Sistan). Some time later he meets and marries Rudabeh, the daughter of the king of Kabul, and Rustam, the hero of all heroes, is born to them. Firdowsi recounts that, through her father, Mihrab of Kabul, Rudabeh is related to Zahhak, the usurper of the Iranian throne.

The stories of Rustam

Simurgh's magic power is soon invoked: at the birth of their child, in his desperation to save Rudabeh from the unbearable pains of childbirth, Zal burns Simurgh's feather. The magic bird immediately appears out of a dark sky and soothingly tells Zal that he will soon be the father of a son 'with the height of a

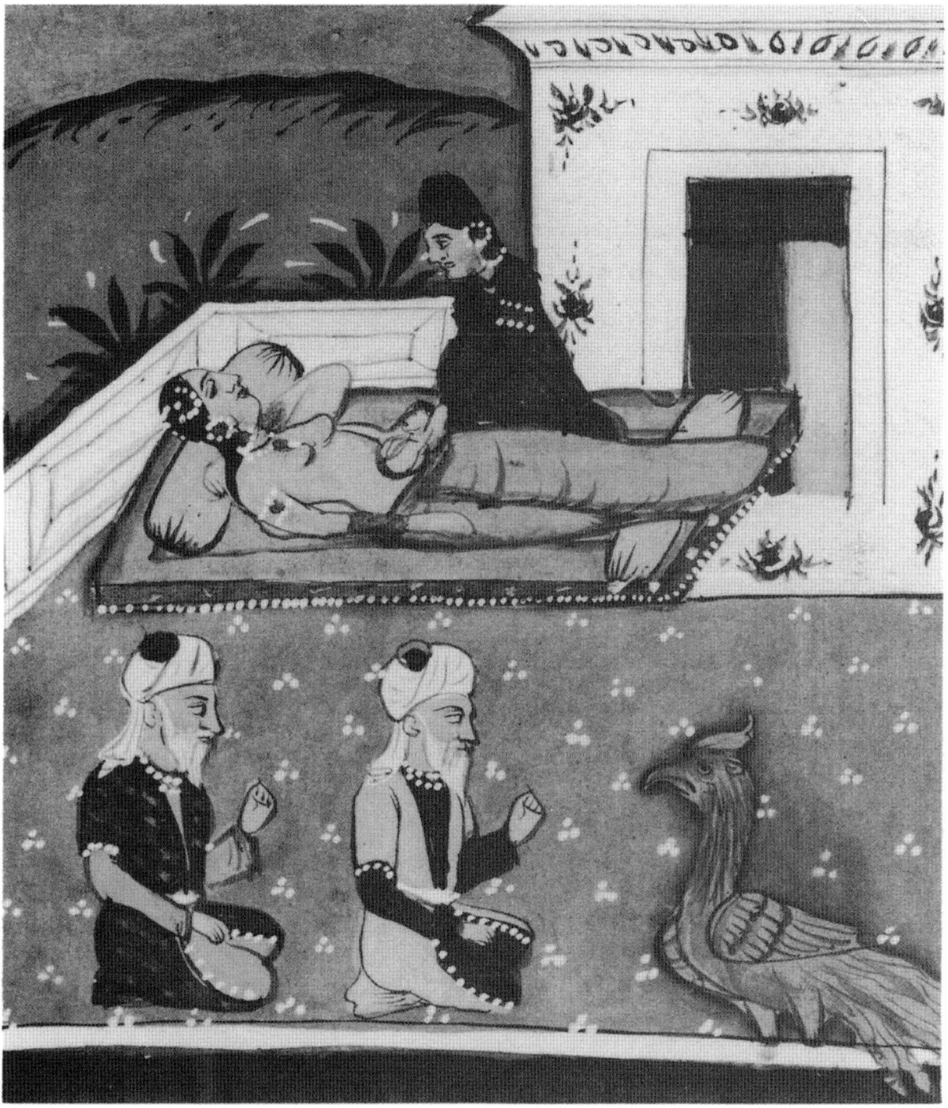

Illustration from an 18th-century Kashmiri abridged prose Shahnameh, showing the birth of Rustam. Sindukht comforts her daughter Rudabeh while Zal and Mihran, the king of Kabul, listen to Simurgh's advice to deliver the baby by Caesarian section.

cypress tree and the strength of an elephant', and that the child is not to be born in the ordinary way but by Caesarian section. The mother recovers fully from her operation with the help of potions prescribed by Simurgh, and by rubbing the feather of the legendary bird on her wound. The boy is named Rustam, of whom it is said that when he was only one day old, you would think he was one year old. Indeed, Rustam develops into a strong lion-like man of such great strength and stature that he has no trouble confronting a roaring elephant and slaying it instantly with his mace. Rustam's heroic deeds and combats are

Page from a 16th-century Shahnameh showing young Rustam, the 'son of a lion', attacking a white elephant and breaking its neck with his bull-headed mace.

numerous, and his bravery and powers are strengthened by the help of his unusual and equally brave horse, Rakhsh. Together they have a series of adventures, including the seven heroic deeds in which they successfully encounter a lion, pass through a waterless desert, confront a dragon, slay a witch and also finally kill *divs*, one of these being the great white demon who had captured Kay Kavus (Kavi Usan of the *Avesta*), the king of kings. Leading an army of other heroes, they restore the royal power and Kay Kavus returns triumphantly to the land of Iran.

Meanwhile, animosity between Iran and Turan continues with Afrasiyab, the king of Turan, taking every opportunity to attack Iran. But because of the bravery of Rustam, the 'hero of the world', and his dedication to the king of kings, the Iranian army usually withstands the attacks. However, it is just this total dedication to Iran and the king of kings that makes Rustam stumble into traps set by Afrasiyab. One of these even causes him to murder his own son, who has come to enthrone him.

While on a hunting adventure near the plains of Turan, Rustam falls asleep and loses his horse Rakhsh. During his search for the horse, he comes to the town of Samangan in enemy country, where the local king takes him in and promises to find Rakhsh. Rustam meets Tahmineh, the king's beautiful daughter, who has fallen in love with him after hearing all the heroic stories about him. Rustam marries Tahmineh, an event greeted with great joy by the king and inhabitants of Samangan. Just before he departs for Iran, Rustam gives his wife a world-famous amulet seal that he wears on his arm. It is to be given to their future child: if a girl, she should wear it in her hair and, if a boy, he should wear it on his arm like his father.

Nine months later Tahmineh gives birth to a son, who is 'like a shining moon, one would say like the elephant-bodied Rustam, or the lion-like Sam'. Named Sohrab by his mother, at one month the boy resembles a year-old child; when he is three years old, he begins learning the art of combat, and by the time he reaches the age of ten, there is no match for him. He soon realises that he is different from and far advanced over other children of his age, and when he asks his mother about his father, she tells him he is the son of Rustam. This prompts Sohrab not only to set off to find his father, but also to cut his ties with Turan, with the intention of removing Kay Kavus as king of kings of Iran and replacing him with his own father. The news of Sohrab's departure soon reaches the ill-willed Afrasiyab, who immediately plans a deadly plot against both father and son: to prevent Sohrab from meeting and knowing his father and, in turn, to keep Rustam in ignorance of his son's identity, so that they will face each other as enemies. Such a combat between father and son, each unknown to the other, would presumably end in Rustam's death at the hands of his offspring. This devious plot is put into action and, like pieces in a chess game, Rustam and Sohrab are moved against each other by outside forces. The tragic twist in the story is poignantly reinforced by the fact that Sohrab suspects that his adversary might be his father, but when he asks the hero for his name, Rustam hides his true identity. Sohrab then tries to learn the truth from the Turanians, but on

Illustration from a Shahnameh of 1649. Rustam kneels, tearing his shirt in grief, beside the dying Sohrab, having just discovered that his opponent is wearing his amulet and is therefore his son. In the foreground are Rustam's leopard cap, bull-headed mace, sword and shield, and at either side attendants hold the heroes' horses.

Afrasiyab's orders they do not reveal Rustam's identity. Only at their final encounter on the battlefield, when Sohrab receives a deadly blow from his father and Rustam discovers his amulet on Sohrab's arm, does Rustam realise that he has slain his own son.

> . . . The two began
> To wrestle, holding by their leathern belts.
> As for Suhrab thou wouldst have said, 'High heaven
> Hath hampered him' while Rustam reaching clutched
> That warrior-leopard by the head and neck,
> Bent down the body of the gallant youth,
> Whose time was come and all whose strength was gone,
> And like a lion dashed him to the ground;
> Then knowing that Suhrab would not stay under,
> Drew lightly from his waist his trenchant sword
> And gashed the bosom of his gallant son.
> (II, v. 502–3)

From Rustam's very long lifetime, spanning the reigns of many kings, comes another tragic story described in the *Shahnameh*, namely that of Siyavush (Siyavarshan of the *Avesta*).

Siyavush is the son of Kay Kavus and a princess descended from Fariydun and the Turanian royal family. As a young boy he is given into the care of Rustam, who teaches him all the princely arts and skills. When he has grown into a handsome man, one of his father's wives, Sudabeh, falls in love with him. When her temptations cannot lure him to deceive his father, she accuses him of treachery and lies to her husband that Siyavush has declared his love for her. Kay Kavus, who initially believes Sudabeh, forgives his son only after he has proved his innocence by dressing in white and riding through fire on a black horse. Passing through fire was an ancient, probably pre-Zoroastrian practice of proving one's innocence.

Siyavush then moves to the court of Afrasiyab, where he falls in love with the king's daughter, Farangis, marries her and settles in the city named after him, Siyavushgird. Afrasiyab's brother Garsivaz, who is jealous of Siyavush, succeeds in turning Afrasiyab against the young prince of Iran, who is then brutally murdered and has his head cut off. Years later, Kay Khusrow (Kavi Haosravah of the *Avesta*), the son of Siyavush, returns from Turan to Iran. After defeating his rival and half-brother, Fariburz, he is hailed as the legitimate heir to his grandfather Kay Kavus and becomes king. Both Garsivaz and Afrasiyab are killed by Kay Khusrow.

After Rustam's victory over the great hero Isfandiyar, whose murder Simurgh has predicted will have tragic consequences, Rustam is himself killed by his half-brother Shaqad and the king of Zabulistan when he falls, with his horse Rakhsh, into the deadly pit they have dug and filled with knives and daggers. Before Rustam dies, however, he succeeds in lifting himself out of the pit and shooting Shaqad with an arrow, pinning his body to a tree trunk.

Illustration from a 14th-century Shahnameh. Rustam shoots Shaqad as Rakhsh lies in the pit.

Fabulous mythological creatures of the Shahnameh

Evil beings in the form of demons or *div* appear side by side with kings and heroes throughout the *Shahnameh*. Firdowsi refers to these demons as bad humans who have not shown gratitude to God. They are often described as the personification of Ahriman, the devil, but they actually represent a specific group of enemy kings from the areas of Mazandaran and Tabaristan, although their exact geographical location is not clear. While the area south of the Caspian Sea in modern Iran is known as Mazandaran, some scholars believe that the original domain was elsewhere, and only in later times was the name transferred to northern Iran. Nevertheless, both personal and place names in northern Iran show the influence of the *div* in this area. For example, a tribe called Div is known to have inhabited Mazandaran in the sixteenth century.

The encounter with the *div* dates from the reign of the first two mythological kings. Siyamak, the son of Kiyumars, first king of the Pishdadian dynasty, is killed by the Black Demon, the son of Ahriman. Then Hushang, Siyamak's son, goes into battle with the Black Demon and avenges his father's murder, confronting the demon with an army composed of fairies, leopards, tigers, lions, wolves and birds. He puts an end to the demon's life by cutting his throat. As already seen, Hushang's son Tahmuras victoriously challenges the demons, and he rides on the back of Ahriman. It is during his rule that the *divs* are finally forced to beg for mercy.

The heroes of the *Shahnameh* usually have to prove their courage and physical strength as well as their utmost allegiance to the king of kings by confronting d*ivs*, dragons, wolves and monsters in different disguises. At the same time, there are also stories about heroes being helped or saved by kind and loving supernatural beings. Among these are Simurgh, the legendary bird, and Rustam's horse, Rakhsh.

Rakhsh

Rakhsh is first mentioned towards the beginning of the *Shahnameh*. Before setting off on a major expedition into the mountains to rescue the king of kings, Kay Qubad, Rustam searches for a suitable horse among all the herds of his native Zabulistan, but none that he tests by pressing his hand on its back can

19th-century painting showing Rustam attacking the 'ugly-faced' black div. Wearing his leopard cap, the hero ties the demon's arms with his lasso.

bear the weight, and their stomachs sag to the ground. Suddenly Rustam spots a mare resembling a lion, with ears sticking out like two daggers. Taking short, quick steps, it is followed by a foal resembling the mother in build, with black eyes, a long tail and hooves like steel. Its light-coloured body has red spots shining like the sun in the sky. Its height equals that of a camel and its strength is like that of an Indian elephant. Rustam is about to use his lasso to capture the foal when he is told by the herdsman not to take someone else's horse. When he asks who the owner is, the herdsman replies that he does not know, but that the foal is known as Rustam's Rakhsh.

Rustam then throws his royal lasso over the head of the foal and is immediately attacked by Rakhsh's mother. But Rustam frightens off the mare by roaring like a lion. When he finally captures Rakhsh and tries to push down its back with one hand, the horse does not move, unaware of the immense pressure on its body. After a ride on Rakhsh, Rustam asks the old herdsman the price of the horse. He is told that the price of this horse is equal to the value of the whole of Iran; so, if he is Rustam, he should go and rescue the country of Iran from its enemies and relieve it from sorrow. Rakhsh remains Rustam's faithful servant and companion until eventually both are killed by Rustam's half-brother.

Rakhsh's extraordinary intelligence and dedication to Rustam are beautifully illustrated in the seven adventures or heroic deeds of Rustam (*haft khan*). To stress the importance of this magnificent horse, Firdowsi refers to him affectionately as 'Rakhsh of all Rakhshes' (*Rakhsh-i Rakhshan*), an echo of such titles as 'king of kings' and 'hero of heroes'. In the first adventure, Rustam lays

ABOVE *Illustration from an 18th-century Kashmiri abridged prose Shahnameh, showing Rustam using his 'royal lasso' to catch Rakhsh.*

Illustration from a 16th-century Shahnameh showing the first stage of Rustam's seven adventures, when Rakhsh kills an attacking lion. The hero, wearing his leopard cap, rests his head on a leopard skin. His bow, quiver and bull-headed mace lie beside him. Rustam is usually described as wearing a babr-i bayan or palangineh, a coat made of leopard skin.

down his sword to take a rest in the reed fields and is unknowingly approached by a lion. 'Boiling like fire', Rakhsh attacks the lion with his forelegs and bites it on the back. When Rustam awakes and sees the dead beast, he reprimands his horse for risking death in the fight, which would have left him without any way of reaching Mazandaran.

In the third of the seven adventures, Rustam has gone to sleep (after an exhausting second adventure, in which thirst has almost killed him and Rakhsh). Before resting, he warns Rakhsh not to fight with lions and dragons. Soon a huge dragon appears, measuring 80 *gaz* (about 80 m) from head to tail. Rakhsh is distressed and tries to awaken his master by pawing the ground with his hooves, but when Rustam opens his eyes, the dragon disappears. Rustam then scolds Rakhsh for disturbing him. The dragon continues with this game, so that each time Rustam is awakened by Rakhsh, he finds only darkness in the wilderness. Finally he threatens to cut off Rakhsh's head. When the dragon reappears once again, breathing fire and smoke, Rakhsh ignores both Rustam's threat and the dragon's disappearing trick and, roaring with excitement and anger, paws the ground until it cracks. This time when the hero awakes, he is able to see the dragon's flames in the darkness. Rakhsh, spellbound until then, attacks the dragon and bites it on the shoulder while Rustam strikes it with his sword and cuts off its head.

Ultimately Rakhsh and Rustam meet their end together, as recounted in the preceding chapter. Even then, when death threatens the great hero, Rakhsh makes a final attempt to rescue his master. Smelling death and danger ahead, he tries in vain to resist bearing Rustam towards the deadly, dagger-filled pits.

Simurgh

The other mythological creature which features throughout the *Shahnameh* as the friend and protector of Rustam and his family is Simurgh, the 'king of birds', who lives at the top of the Alburz Mountains and raises Rustam's father Zal. Zal's Simurgh is also called upon for help when Rustam is fighting Isfandiyar, in the famous encounter between the two equals. Badly injured, Rustam for the first time doubts whether he can withstand Isfandiyar's power, and he asks his father for help. Zal, shocked by the desperate physical condition of both Rustam and Rakhsh, sets alight the feather Simurgh has given him.

Immediately the dark sky turns darker and Simurgh emerges. She listens to Zal's description of the hero's deep wounds. Firdowsi describes how Simurgh first praises Isfandiyar's divine lineage and heroic status and cannot understand why Rustam has confronted him. However, she soon sees to Rustam, pulling eight arrows out of his body and rubbing her feathers over the wounds. She then sees to Rakhsh:

> She in like manner having called for Rakhsh
> Employed her beak on him to make him whole,
> And drew out from his neck six arrow-heads.
> (v, v. 1704)

19th-century Qajar illustration in a 15th-century Shahnameh, showing Rustam shooting Isfandiyar in the eye with his forked arrow.

Simurgh makes it clear that she disapproves of Rustam fighting with Isfandiyar, who is of royal and divine descent,

> a holy man who hath the Grace of God.
> (V, v. 1705)

He is the son of Gushtasp (Vishtaspa of the *Avesta)*, the patron of Zoroaster, and he has been made invulnerable by Zoroaster. But despite her disapproval of the fight, Simurgh reveals to Rustam the secret of overcoming Isfandiyar, once again proving her loyalty to Zal and his son. The magic bird tells Rustam to prepare a special shaft with three feathers and two arrow heads, and to aim it towards Isfandiyar's eyes. Rustam follows Simurgh's advice, although before discharging the deadly arrow he suggests to Isfandiyar that they should end their conflict. Isfandiyar, however, still convinced that no one is equal to him, refuses, and thus finally falls victim to Rustam.

It is interesting that, in another story about the hero Isfandiyar (who also has seven adventures), Firdowsi describes how Isfandiyar fights a large monstrous bird, also called Simurgh though obviously not the same one as Zal's protective guardian, and through cunning he defeats her, finally cutting the vicious bird to pieces with his sword. Firdowsi then describes how the earth was covered in feathers from mountain to mountain.

Illustration from an 18th-century Kashmiri abridged prose Shahnameh, depicting Isfandiyar emerging from his ingenious box to kiss a vicious bird (also called Simurgh).

Battling with the demons

The last of Rustam's seven heroic deeds in Mazandaran introduces demons such as Arjang and the Div-e Sepid (white demon), the latter being the arch-demon who has captured the king. The *divs* of Mazandaran, who were enemies of the Iranians, looked like demons in that they were large and often furry, but they also possessed human-like qualities. The sorrow of captivity as well as the ugliness and bad temper of the white demon has caused blindness in Kay Qubad, and Rustam is told that the only way to restore the king's eyesight is to kill the white demon and apply three drops of its blood to the king's eyes. As Rustam rides on the wind-like Rakhsh towards the cave of the great *div*, he encounters a whole army of demons asleep in the heat of the sun. When he finally makes his way into the darkness of the cave, he finds the great white demon at rest. Awoken by Rustam's leopard-like roaring, the *div* appears 'like a black mountain', but receives a heavy blow that cuts off an arm and a leg. The white demon continues its struggle with only one leg until, after a long and bloody fight, Rustam lifts it up, throws it to the ground, and cuts out its liver with his dagger. Having witnessed the battle, the other demons flee. The blood of the white demon is applied and the king miraculously regains his sight.

The story of Akvan, one of the most famous demons, is told in great detail by Firdowsi. This demon attacks the royal herd in the shape of a wild ass, but acts like a male lion by breaking the horses' heads. Kay Khusrow, the king of Iran, knows immediately that this unlikely wild ass could only be Akvan, and

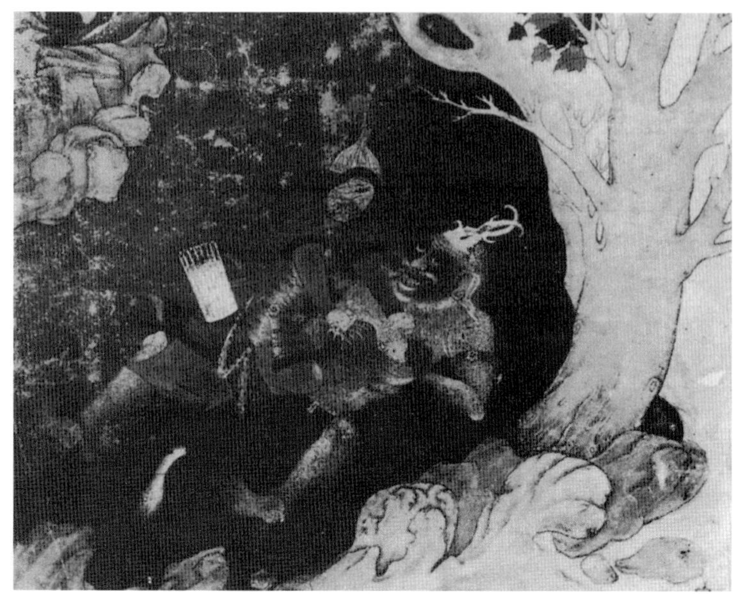

Illustration from a late 16th-century Shahnameh showing the seventh and final stage of Rustam's adventures. The hero kills the Div-e Sepid (white demon) and, with the blood from its heart, cures King Kay Kavus' temporary blindness.

BELOW *Illustrations from a 16th-century Shahnameh. The demon Akvan carries the sleeping Rustam, prior to throwing him into the sea. The fully armed hero is wearing his leopard cap while his bow, quiver and bull-headed mace are lying beside him.*

sends for Rustam to come to Zabulistan. On reading the royal command, the hero of heroes hastens to reassure the king that 'whether demon, lion or a male dragon, it will not escape my sharp sword'. Rustam arrives on the scene resembling 'a male lion, holding a lasso in his hand and riding on a dragon' (Rakhsh). He seeks the demon for three days, until on the fourth day he sees it passing by like 'the north wind'. Akvan is described as shining like gold on the outside, but ugly beneath. Protruding like a snake from its skin, its head resembles that of an elephant with long hair. Its mouth is filled with teeth like the tusks of a boar. Its eyes are white and its lips black.

Rustam's attempt to catch the wild ass which is Akvan proves unsuccessful, as every time he throws his lasso, the beast manages to disappear as effortlessly as the wind. Even his arrows do not reach the demon and finally, exhausted by his efforts, Rustam dismounts, unsaddles Rakhsh, takes off his leopard skin, puts down his arrows and lasso, and lies down to rest on the felt underlay of the saddle. It is only then that Akvan, watching from afar, turns into a howling wind, changes the earth into dust, and suddenly lifts Rustam into the sky. When Rustam wakes up, he finds himself trapped, and for once his mighty strength, his sword and mace are powerless, for Akvan is even stronger and more powerful. There then follows an interesting conversation while the demon carries the hero in a flight across the sky. Akvan is planning to drop Rustam either on to the mountains or into the ocean, and he asks the hero which he would prefer. Rustam's sharp intelligence gives him an insight into the character of the demon, so he decides not to tell his true wish, which is for the chance to swim out of the ocean. He therefore beseeches Akvan not to drop him into the ocean, saying souls cannot ascend from its watery depths to heaven, and pleading to be thrown instead on to the mountains among the leopards and the lions. On hearing Rustam's plea, Akvan casts him into the ocean, just as Rustam had divined, and the hero reaches shore safely by fending off the sharks with his right arm, dagger and leg while swimming with his left arm and leg. Rustam then finds Rakhsh and, mounted on his great steed, meets Akvan once again for a final encounter near a water source. This time Akvan asks Rustam whether he has not had enough of battles, he who has escaped the ocean and the jaws of sharks, returning to the plains barely half alive. Rustam replies with a roar like a lion, unties his lasso from his saddle strap, and throws it around the demon's waist. After tying the lasso on to the saddle he turns around, lifts his mace like a blacksmith's hammer, and hits Akvan on the head. Then he hacks off the demon's head with his dagger.

Encounters with dragons

As mentioned above, one of the mythological creatures which Rustam and his horse Rakhsh encounter during their third adventure is a dragon who hides from the hero in the darkness and is finally attacked by Rakhsh before Rustam cuts off its head with his sword. But perhaps one of the most dramatic combats between a human and a dragon appears in the parallel story of Isfandiyar in his

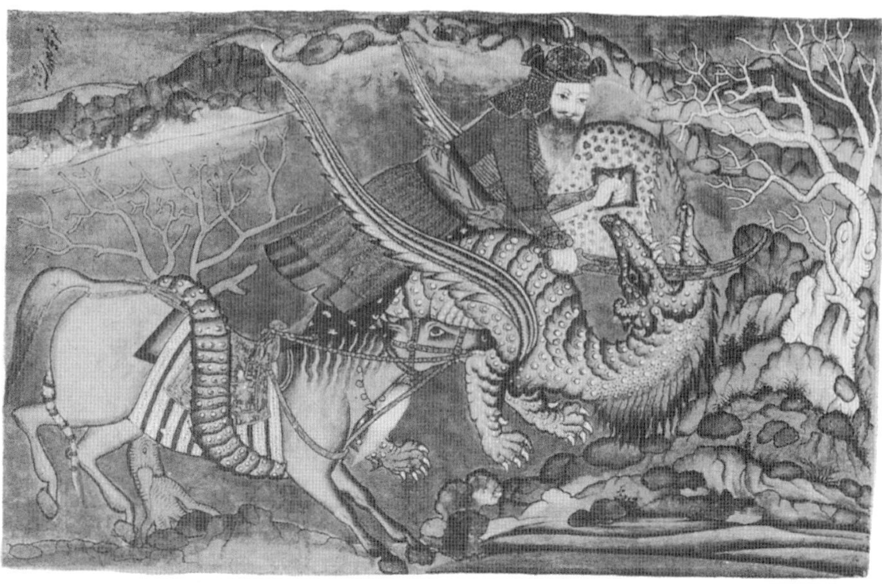

Illustration from an 18th-century Shahnameh showing the fully armed Rustam with his leopard-skin shield attacking the huge dragon while the monster's long tail is coiled around Rakhsh. Trees and mountains indicate the wooded landscape of Mazandaran.

own third adventure. Having already successfully slain wolves and lions and an evil bird, he is faced by a fearsome dragon, described as resembling a black mountain which blots out the sun and the moon. The beast's eyes are said to be like two shining pools of blood, and fire bursts out of its mouth which, when open, looks like a deep dark cave. Before setting out, Isfandiyar devises a most ingenious wooden structure (similar to that used in his battle of wits with the vicious bird). He orders his carpenters to build him a wooden box covered with sharp spikes. This is placed on a wheeled cart pulled by two valuable horses, and Isfandiyar hides inside the box. When the dragon attacks, it swallows the horses and the cart, but the spikes keep the box (with the hero inside) lodged in the monster's throat until a green sea of poison oozes out of the dragon's mouth. Isfandiyar climbs out of the deadly box and sticks a sharp-pointed sword into the dragon's head, splitting open its brain.

> . . . in the dragon's gullet stuck
> The sword blades, and blood poured forth like a sea;
> It could not free its gullet, for the swords
> Were sheathed within it. Tortured by the points
> And chariot the dragon by degrees
> Grew weak, and then the gallant warrior,
> Arising from the box, clutched his keen glaive
> With lion-grip and hacked the dragon's brains
> Till fumes of venom rising from the dust
> O'erpowered him; he tumbled mountain-like
> And swooned away.
> (V, v. 1593)

Stories of Zoroaster, Cyrus and Alexander

Historical figures often enter the world of myths, with legends embroidering the original details of their lives to such an extent that it often becomes difficult to separate fact from fiction.

Zoroaster

Legends surround the birth of the prophet Zoroaster, and later Zoroastrian texts such as the *Denkard* describe how the Divine Glory (*khvarnah*) and the guarding spirit (*fravahr*) were already present inside the prophet's mother. The Divine Glory originated from the world of light of the sun, moon and stars, and found its way from there to the family hearth in the home of Zoroaster's ancestors. Thus Zoroaster's mother, Dughdov, carried inside her body the Divine Glory, which was so bright that it made her shine in the darkness. This illuminating effect was exploited by evil demons to suggest that the girl was a witch, so her father sent her away. She stayed with the head of the Spitama family and later married the son, Purushasp. One day after the two are married, Purushasp is guided by some of the immortals to a special tree. The guarding spirit, having been brought from heaven to earth, has been placed in its branches in the shape of the haoma plant. He takes the plant back to his wife. Zoroaster's physical body (*tan gohr*) actually reaches his mother through the milk of young cows which have been fed on plants nourished in turn by special rainwater made to fall by the lords of waters and plants, Khurdad and Amurdad. Dughdov drinks the mixture of the crushed haoma plant and the milk.

Myths also surround the time after Zoroaster's birth, concerning the demons' continued efforts to show that the Divine Glory is an evil sign. As a result, Zoroaster's father makes several attempts to put an end to his son's life: he tries to burn him in a fire, and he places him in front of stampeding cattle, and then horses. But each time the child is saved: in the first instance, the fire will not start, and in the second and third, a bull and a stallion respectively stand guard over him. He is even abandoned in the wilderness, but a she-wolf rescues him and a ewe suckles the newborn baby.

More legends exist in the *Denkard* and much later stories about the prophet's efforts to convert King Vishtaspa to Zoroastrianism. They describe how the prophet is thrown into prison, but succeeds in gaining his release by curing one of the king's horses. When Vishtaspa finally accepts the new religion, his wish to foresee his fate is granted. By drinking a special mixture containing haoma juice, he falls unconscious and sees himself in heaven. Other wishes are also granted to those nearest to Vishtaspa: one of his sons drinks a cup of milk which makes him immortal; his minister Jamasp gains knowledge by inhaling perfumes; and Vishtaspa's other son, Isfandiyar, eats a pomegranate and thereby becomes invincible.

Cyrus the Great

Cyrus the Great, founder of the Achaemenid empire, came to power after deposing the Median king Astyages in 550 BC. After a series of victories over the Lydian king, Croesus, in 547 or 546 BC, and after his successful campaign against the Babylonians in 539 BC, Cyrus established a large empire stretching from the Mediterranean in the west to eastern Iran, and from the Black Sea in the north to Arabia. He was killed in 530 BC during a campaign in the north-eastern part of his empire.

The legend of Cyrus and the myths surrounding his birth are best described by Herodotus, the Greek historian of the mid-fourth century BC, who lived in Asia Minor. According to him, Astyages was Cyrus' maternal grandfather, who dreamt that his daughter Mandane produced so much water that it overran his city and the whole of Asia. When the holy men (*magi*) hear of the king's dream, they warn him of its consequences. As a result, her father gives Mandane in marriage to a Persian called Cambyses who, although of noble descent, is considered by Astyages to be 'much lower than a Mede of middle estate'. Mandane and Cambyses have not been married a year when Astyages once again has a dream, this time that a vine growing from inside Mandane's womb will spread all over Asia. The *magi* immediately see a bad omen and tell the king that Mandane's son will usurp his throne. The king sends for his pregnant daughter and keeps her under tight guard until the child is born. Royal instructions are given to Harpagus, a Median nobleman and confidant of the king, that he should kill and dispose of the newly born child. But at that moment fate and supernatural forces intervene and Harpagus decides not to kill the baby himself. Instead, he calls for a royal herdsman and orders him to carry out the king's command, adding that he will be severely punished if the child is allowed to live. As it happens, the herdsman's own wife has given birth to a stillborn child during her husband's absence, and she pleads with him to keep the royal baby and regard it as their own. They bury the body of their own dead child and look after the infant Cyrus as their own flesh and blood.

Cyrus soon develops into an outstanding young boy, overshadowing his friends and showing royal qualities of leadership. It is reported that, during a game with other children, Cyrus is chosen to play king. Promptly assuming this role, he metes out harsh punishment to the son of a distinguished Mede who refuses to take orders from him. The father of the badly beaten boy complains to King Astyages, who in turn calls for Cyrus in order to have him punished. When asked why he has behaved in such a savage manner, Cyrus defends his action by

The famous clay cylinder of Cyrus the Great, written in Babylonian cuneiform, recording his capture of Babylon in 539 BC.

explaining that, because he was playing the role of king, he had every reason to punish someone who was not obeying his command. Astyages knows immediately that these are not the words of a herdsman's son and realises that the boy is his own grandson, the son of Mandane. The story is confirmed by the herdsman, albeit with great reluctance. Astyages punishes Harpagus for his disobedience by serving him the cooked remains of his own son's body at a royal dinner. Then, on the advice of the *magi*, the king allows Cyrus to return to Persia to his real parents.

Meanwhile Harpagus burns with feelings of revenge against Astyages and decides to encourage Cyrus to seize his grandfather's throne. Suggesting this plan to Cyrus is not easy, as it has to be sent to him in Persia. Herodotus describes how Harpagus writes his plan on a piece of paper and inserts it into the belly of a slain hare which has not yet been skinned. The skin is sewn up and the hare given to a trusted servant who, posing as a hunter, travels to Persia and presents Cyrus with the hare, telling him to cut open the dead animal. After reading Harpagus' letter, Cyrus begins to play with the idea of seizing power from Astyages. As part of a careful plan, he persuades a number of the Persian tribes to side with him to throw off the yoke of Astyages and the Medes. Cyrus succeeds in overthrowing his grandfather and becomes the ruler of the united Medes and Persians.

This fascinating account by Herodotus is still regarded as the most reliable source on Cyrus' birth and coming to power, although it has a strong mythological flavour. Other descriptions, such as that of Xenophon, the Greek who served more than a hundred years later in the army of Cyrus the Younger, and the accounts of the Greek physician Ctesias in the fourth century BC, are usually considered less reliable. Among the later sources, however, one story is of particular interest. It describes how the baby Cyrus, abandoned in the woods by a shepherd, is fed by a dog until the shepherd returns with his wife and takes the infant into their care. This tale is very much in line with mythological stories surrounding the infancy of other heroes and rulers. For example, Romulus and Remus, the twins who founded Rome, were saved and raised by a wolf, and Zal, Rustam's father, was brought up by the legendary bird Simurgh.

Stories of prophetic dreams like those of Astyages, and of the abandonment of newborn babies, recur consistently in Iranian mythology. Darab, the father of Dara (Darius III), in the *Shahnameh* is said to be abandoned by his mother Humay, only returning to his natural mother when he is grown up. In the story of the birth and upbringing of Kay Khusrow, the Kiyanian king and son of Prince Siyavush, some of the mythological elements are also reminiscent of the story of Cyrus. Kay Khusrow is born in Turan at the court of King Afrasiyab, the opponent of the Iranians. Before being murdered, his father sees in a dream that Kay Khusrow will become the ruler of Iran. When the child is born, he is put in the care of shepherds and his true identity is kept secret. Meanwhile, Gudarz, the great Iranian hero, sees in a dream a cloud full of water ascending from Iran, and an angel informs him of the existence of a new king called Kay Khusrow. Gudarz then sends his son Giv to find Kay Khusrow and bring him back to Iran.

Another story in the *Shahnameh* that has been linked with the legend of Cyrus is that of Ardashir, the founder of the Sasanian dynasty. Ardashir's father, Sasan, is claimed to have been a descendant of the Achaemenid rulers of Iran. The young Sasan works as a shepherd for Babak (Papak), the local king of Fars in south-western Iran. One night Babak has a dream in which Sasan is riding on a huge white elephant with everyone saluting him. He also sees the sacred fires of the Zoroastrians burning in front of Sasan. After consulting his wise men, who tell him that the young man in his dream will become the king, Babak takes in Sasan and gives him his daughter in marriage. The offspring of this union is Ardashir, who defeats the last Parthian king, Ardavan, in AD 224. An almost identical story appears in the *Karnamak-i Artakhshir-i Papakan* (*Deedbook of Ardashir, Son of Babak*), of the Sasanian period dating from the seventh century, which probably was known to Firdowsi. It has been suggested that the idea of the mythological birth of Cyrus the Great was used in stories and legends about other great rulers, and that the resemblance of the Kay Khusrow tale to the Cyrus myth may indicate that Cyrus and Kay Khusrow were the same person.

Alexander the Great

Persian legends were also created around the figure of Alexander the Great, who defeated Dara or Darius III, the last Achaemenid king, in 331 BC. It is surprising, but not impossible to explain, that this foreign conqueror should be hailed as a great man. Although he was a usurper, Alexander entered Persian literature and historical accounts as a great statesman and philosopher, and it is only occasionally that negative aspects of his character or evil deeds are described in the sources. One such instance is in Firdowsi's description of the famous *taqdis*, the mythical throne of the Iranian kings. This says that, until the time of Alexander's conquest, each king had added to the splendour of the throne, but Alexander broke the throne into pieces. It was not until the rule of Khusrow Parviz (Khusrow II, AD 590–628) that the throne was restored. Tabari, the great historian of the tenth century, mentions Alexander in connection with the burning of the *Avesta*, which was considered a most wicked deed. None the less, Alexander has entered national Iranian epics as a hero and the legitimate heir to

Illustration from a late 15th-century Khamseh of Nizami, showing Alexander comforting the dying Dara (Darius III).

the throne. Such legitimacy must have been a political necessity, as only rulers with a genuine right to the Kingly Glory were chosen to rule over Iran. A foreign usurper would have no place in the country's history, and in order to make Alexander qualify, the *Shahnameh* regards him as the half-brother of the last Achaemenid king.

The most important biography of Alexander, the *Pseudo-Callisthenes*, which probably dates from the third century AD, was the original source of information on the Macedonian ruler. Translations into other languages, including Pahlavi and then Arabic, provided the necessary source material for later romances on Alexander. Among these are Firdowsi's description of Alexander in his *Shahnameh* of the early eleventh century and Nizami Ganjavi's *Iskandarnameh* (*Book of Alexander*), also a poetic work but written in the twelfth century.

Firdowsi clearly used two different sources for the character of Alexander in the *Shahnameh*. In the main section on Alexander, the poet describes him as an Iranian prince of the Kiyanian line, with a legitimate claim to the Iranian throne and the Divine Glory. But later, when writing about the Sasanian period and Ardashir, its first ruler, he launches into a fierce attack on Alexander, describing him as an enemy of Iran, as evil and destructive as Zahhak, the usurper of the Iranian throne, and as Afrasiyab, the Turanian. He also accuses Alexander of having destroyed the Iranian throne and condemns him. Nizami, on the other hand, takes a more philosophical approach to Alexander's rule, and his *Iskandarnameh* portrays Alexander as the ultimate and perfect ruler.

In the first part of his work, known as the *Sharafnameh*, Nizami describes the birth of Alexander. The poet gives two different versions, but adds that there were others as well. The first story describes Alexander's mother as being from Rum (Greece), and relates that when the devout woman becomes pregnant she leaves her town and her husband in distress. She gives birth to her child alone among some ruins, and then dies, leaving the baby unattended. It so happens that the king, Philphius/Philqus (Philip of Macedon), is hunting in the plains and passes the dead woman. He sees the hungry newborn infant sucking his finger and takes the baby with him, raising him as his own son and making him his crown prince. Here Nizami comments that neither this version nor the one told by Firdowsi, in which Alexander is related to Dara, the Iranian king, is true, and that Alexander was actually the son of Philip. Nizami then gives his second version, in which he describes at great length how Philip falls in love with a beautiful woman of his court, who becomes pregnant by him. The king orders the wise men to read the stars and tell him of any secrets they reveal about the unborn baby. The stars indicate strength, courage, wisdom and the absence of the evil eye, and also show that the baby will be presented with the key to the world. The royal birth is therefore celebrated with much rejoicing. Soon after starting to walk 'gracefully like a pheasant', the young Alexander asks his wetnurse for a bow and arrow and practices target shooting, sometimes at paper and other times at silk. Once grown, he takes up a sword and fights with lions. Then he discovers the joys of riding and follows the path of kingship. Alexander is taught by Aristotle's father and then learns the skills of warfare. After the death of his father, he ascends the Macedonian throne, defeats the Iranian king, Dara, and becomes the ruler of Iran. He then marries Roxana (Rushanak), the daughter of the deposed Dara, and travels across his realm eastwards to India and China. He also visits the Ka'aba, the holy place of the Muslims, and finally returns to Greece, his birthplace.

In the second part of his epic, the *Iqbalnameh*, Nizami elevates Alexander above even the status of world conqueror, to that of philosopher and prophet. Again and again Nizami defends the accuracy of his version, describing at great length Alexander's knowledgeable involvement in philosophy and science. He recounts that, before his death, Alexander divides up his realm among his feudal lords, who thus become independent and need not take orders from each other. This does in fact closely follow the historical facts.

Nizami offers various suggestions as to how Alexander acquired his title of 'the two-horned' (*dhulqarnain*, Persian *zulqarnain*), a title also mentioned in the Qur'an but not necessarily in connection with Alexander. One is that Alexander saw the dawn in both east and west, *qarn* in Arabic meaning the upper edge of the sun. It was also said that in a dream Alexander saw the east and west take the sky away from the sun, or that he lived for two *qarn* (*qarn* also meaning time, a generation). Another suggestion is that he wore his hair in two plaits at the back (*qarn* can also mean a lock of hair in Arabic). Still another, according to a well-known source, has it that in a Greek portrait Alexander was shown flanked by two horned angels, and that one horn (*qarn*) of each angel seemed to be

Obverse of a coin of Lysimachus of Thrace (306–281 BC), showing Alexander with a ram's horn.

protruding from the sides of the ruler's own head, suggesting that Alexander was divine, chosen by God, and that the angels are there to protect him. This portrait was passed around the kingdom, and the Arabs may have believed that the horns belonged to Alexander himself. There is an interesting parallel here with religious beliefs in ancient Mesopotamia, where a divinity was signified by a horned head-dress. But Alexander's title seems to have derived from a connection with the Egyptian god Zeus-Amun, who is often associated with a ram. After conquering Egypt Alexander was declared the son of Zeus-Amun, and on some Hellenistic coins he is shown with a ram's horn on his head.

Nizami then goes on to relate an amusing anecdote on the same subject. The tale is that Alexander had very large ears, which he kept hidden beneath his gold crown. Only the slave who shaved his head knew his secret, but when this slave died he had to be replaced. The new hairdresser arrives and is immediately warned by the king to keep his large ears a secret. If he does not, Alexander threatens to give the slave a good 'ear-rubbing' and kill him. In his fright the poor slave practically loses the power of speech altogether. Carrying the burden of such a great secret finally makes him ill and one day he leaves the palace, driven by despair into the fields. There he sees a deep well and, putting his head into it, he shouts down into the depths that the king of the world has long ears. He then returns in relief to the palace.

Once the slave has gone away, a bamboo stick containing the secret emerges from inside the well. A passing shepherd sees the bamboo stick and takes it to make a flute. One day when Alexander is riding through the fields, he hears a song about his big ears coming out of the shepherd's flute. He questions the shepherd, who recounts how he found the stick and made it into a flute. Alexander realises that his slave has somehow revealed his secret, and accosts the poor man for an explanation. Knowing that he must tell the truth even if it costs him his life, the slave explains that he had been unable to bear the burden of his secret alone and so chose what he thought would be a safe receptacle for it. Alexander forgives the slave, realising that no one can be forced to keep a secret and that, in the end, all secrets will be revealed.

Continuation of an ancient tradition

It is not unusual to find, in many of the written works already mentioned, references to the sources used for ancient stories. These sources were both written and spoken, the latter being part of an ancient oral tradition passed on from generation to generation. The Zoroastrian priests, for example, had to learn religious hymns and prayers by heart and repeat them word for word. The sacred words of the prophet Zoroaster, the *Gatha*, and other parts of the *Avesta*, were preserved by word of mouth until as late as the fourteenth or fifteenth century AD. The fact that the holy book of the Zoroastrians was kept alive in such a manner proves the importance and long history of oral tradition.

In addition to the Zoroastrian priests who kept their religion alive by memorising and repeating the hymns and prayers, there were also minstrels (*ramishgar, khuniyagar*) who performed for the ruler and his court. The existence of such minstrels is mentioned in the works of many poets. The origin of the ancient stories is usually ascribed to the Sasanian period, which began in the third century AD and ended with the advent of Islam. Many of them actually date from an even earlier time, but 'Sasanian' seems to have become a general term for everything pre-Islamic.

Sometimes the figure of a minstrel is built into the story as told by the poet, and the minstrel's songs add to its development. This is certainly the case in the love story of Vis and Ramin, which is of ancient origin. In it Ramin, himself an accomplished minstrel (*gusan*) and harp player, sings about his and Vis' love. The poet Gurgani starts by giving the reader valuable information about the origin of this love story:

> A popular story in this country or the world, it was arranged by six wise men . . . but its language was Pahlavi [Middle Persian] which is not known and understood by everyone. This was used in this country by those who were studying this language.

This indicates that, at the time of Gurgani in the middle of the eleventh century, a written version in the older language of Pahlavi was available, but a Persian translation must also have existed. The Persian prose version was turned into a romantic poem by Gurgani. He says that, although a myth can be excellent and sweet, it can be improved through rhyme and metre.

The art of storytelling was highly regarded in ancient Iran, and the names of some of the most accomplished and highly acclaimed storytellers have

Illustration from a 16th-century (1539–43) Khamseh of Nizami showing Barbad, the 'king of minstrels', performing on the lute at the court of Khusrow II.

survived in later literature. Often they sang their tales and accompanied themselves on a musical instrument. Bahram Gur (Bahram V, 420–38), the renowned Sasanian king whose bravery, love of hunting, and unrivalled archery skill are widely celebrated in poetry and art, had as his favourite slave a Greek girl, Azadeh, who sang and played the harp. She accompanied him on his hunting expeditions. Bahram once asked the king of India to send him ten thousand male and female minstrels and harpists.

Such references to minstrels are numerous in the *Shahnameh*, the most detailed being the story of Barbad, who is highly praised by both Firdowsi and Nizami. He eventually becomes the king of minstrels at the court of the Sasanian king Khusrow II (AD 590–628), known as Khusrow Parviz. Barbad decides to challenge Sarkash, the reigning court minstrel, but is banned from the royal entourage. Determined to attract the king's attention, Barbad goes to the royal gardens and makes friends with the gardener, who promises to tell him when the king of kings is coming to the gardens. One day Barbad is informed that the king is expected to visit the royal gardens. The minstrel dresses himself in green and dyes his musical instrument green, then hides in a tree. The king arrives and makes himself comfortable. Barbad then begins to sing. The king and his followers are delighted with his beautiful voice and wonder who the singer of such a sweet tune could be. Sarkash faints at the realisation that only Barbad, his rival, could play and sing in such a way. The king orders his entourage to look for the singer, but they are unable to find him in his green camouflage. After another song and another fruitless search, the king manages to lure

Barbad out of hiding by promising to fill his mouth and lap with gems. On hearing these words, Barbad descends from the tree and introduces himself to Khusrow Parviz as his slave, who lives only to sing for him. Barbad is greatly rewarded and replaces Sarkash, the previous court minstrel, becoming the king of minstrels (*shah-i ramishgaran*). When Khusrow Parviz is later murdered, Barbad cuts off his fingers and burns his musical instruments as an expression of devotion.

Minstrels at the courts of kings combined the skills of poets and musicians. It was a privilege to be a minstrel at the royal court, as shown in the story of Barbad. A similarly high status was enjoyed by the first great Persian poet, Rudaki, who lived in the early tenth century. Mentioned in many Islamic sources and hailed as the 'king of poets', the blind Rudaki sang his poems to the accompaniment of harp and lute.

Vis and Ramin

The story of Vis and Ramin dates from the pre-Islamic period. The poet Gurgani used the theme in the mid-eleventh century and claimed a Sasanian origin for it. Now, however, it is regarded as belonging to the Parthian period, probably the first century AD. It has also been suggested that Gurgani's story reflects the traditions and customs of the period immediately before he himself lived. This cannot be ruled out, as stories retold from ancient sources often include elements drawn from the time of their narrator.

The framework of the story is the opposition of two Parthian ruling houses, one in the west and the other in the east. The existence of these small kingdoms and the feudalistic background point to a date in the Parthian period. The popularity of this pre-Islamic story in the Islamic period is mentioned by the poet himself, and shows that there was a demand for ancient themes and traditional lore.

The plot unfolds as a struggle over love and honour between two ruling families. Instead of the Kavi kings of the *Avesta* and the Kiyanian rulers of the *Shahnameh*, one set of protagonists is from the house of Qaren (the Parthian noble family of Karen). In the story their seat of power is the ancient city of Hamadan in Media. Their opponent is Mubad Manikan, the king of Merv (now in Turkmenistan in Central Asia), who rules in the east. The poem begins with Mubad, the old king of Merv, declaring his love for Shahru, the beautiful 'fairy-faced' queen of Mah (Media). Shahru explains to Mubad that she is already married and has a son, Viru, but she has to promise that, if she ever has a daughter, she will give her to Mubad as his wife. Shahru agrees to this because she does not believe she will ever bear another child. The oath is sealed with a handshake and written down on silk. However, it so happens that 'the dried-up tree turned green and came out with a hundred leaves and flowers. In her old age Shahru became pregnant, like a pearl fallen into an oyster'.

The baby is a girl, whom they call Vis. She is immediately given into the care of a wetnurse who takes her to Khuzistan and brings her up with the other child in her care. This is Ramin, younger brother of the king of Merv. When the children grow up, Ramin is called back to Merv and Vis is sent back to her home in Hamadan. Her mother, Shahru, decides that the only man in Iran worthy of such beauty and culture is her son Viru, Vis' own brother. When their stars are consulted and the omens are found positive, a wedding of great splendour takes place. It is during these festivities that Zard, a half-brother of King Mubad, arrives at court to deliver a message reminding Shahru of her promise to give him her daughter's hand. Vis refuses to leave her brother-husband and Mubad in fury determines to go to war with the house of Qaren. He sends messengers to many places and finds much support among their kings, including those of Tabaristan, Gurgan, Dahistan, Khorezmia, Sogdia, Sind, India, Tibet and China. Soon his court is filled with the commanders of armies and the plains of Merv are crowded with people, resembling the Day of Judgement. Meanwhile, Shahru enlists the support of the kings who attended the wedding: those of Azerbaijan, Ray, Gilan, Khuzistan, Istakhr and Isfahan, all in the western part of Iran. The two armies meet on the plains of Nihavand, and Vis' father is killed on the battlefield. Meanwhile, Ramin catches a glimpse of Vis, his childhood friend, and instantly falls in love with her. He tries to persuade his older brother, the king, to give up the idea of marrying Vis, but Mubad's love grows even stronger and he is determined to have her as his wife. Mubad finally succeeds in persuading Shahru to let him marry her daughter by giving her precious gifts, reminding her of their oath, and asking her not to turn her back on the Almighty. In fear of God, Shahru opens the gate of the fortress and lets Mubad take Vis away with him.

While celebrations are under way in the city of Merv, Ramin is sick with love for Vis. She, for her part, is determined to use her father's death as an excuse not to allow Mubad to get close to her. At this point, an unexpected character arrives on the scene to control their destiny: the nurse who had

Pottery plaque with a scene of performing acrobats, probably Sasanian.

Silver plate showing a ban scene. The reclining king wears a crown and diaden and rests on a bench throne (takht). The musician playing a harp is also singing. Late Sasanian, probably 8th century AD.

brought up Vis and Ramin hurries to Merv to be near Vis. Using mysterious powers, she arranges a meeting between her two former charges, which leads to an unfulfilled but passionate love affair. At the same time Mubad, whom Vis has kept distant, pines for his young and beautiful wife. She and Ramin, torn between their love for each other and their feelings of guilt towards Mubad, seem like helpless figures manipulated by destiny. Through the devious plots of the nurse, the two young people finally consummate their love during Mubad's absence from Merv.

Unaware of the affair between his wife and his younger brother, Mubad invites them both to join him in the western highlands and suggests that Vis should visit her family. Mubad then overhears a conversation between the nurse and Vis, revealing her liaison with Ramin. Mad with rage, he threatens to expose Vis and kill Ramin, but Vis manages to turn his rage away, declaring that he means more to her than anyone else. Viru, Vis' brother and first husband, cannot understand her passion for Ramin. He reminds her of her noble lineage and urges her not to shame her ancestors by her infatuation. Vis and Ramin finally flee to Ray, keeping their whereabouts a secret, but when Ramin writes a letter to his mother she betrays him to Mubad. On their return to Merv, the lovers continue their secret meetings, using every opportunity to be together behind the old king's back. He is haunted by the thought of his wife's infidelity and his brother's deception, and he locks her away in an isolated fortress during his absences from court.

By now Vis' and Ramin's liaison is well known in Merv and, during a court banquet, Ramin (himself an accomplished minstrel and harp player) sings of their love. Mubad, infuriated by this openness, threatens to cut Ramin's throat. When Ramin defends himself, the king comes to his senses and stays his hand. Torn between his love for Vis and his loyalty to Mubad, Ramin listens to the advice of a wise man, who tells him that he has come under the spell of a demon and that, if he goes out into the world, he will find many women more truthful and virtuous than Vis. Ramin decides to leave Merv and start a new life, moving westwards after being granted the kingdoms of Ray and Gurgan.

In the west Ramin meets and falls in love with Gul, a Parthian princess, and marries her, finally forgetting his old love. His days of pleasure and love with Gul come to an end, however, when one day he compares her with Vis and suggests that she is like an apple cut in half. Gul, upset to be compared with Ramin's lover, considers this a betrayal. Reminded once again of Vis, Ramin writes her a letter and a long correspondence begins between the two former lovers.

Ramin returns to Merv, where he and Vis are reunited. They escape together, taking with them the king's treasures. Once again, their journey takes them to the west and, after travelling through Qazvin, they settle in Daylaman. When Mubad discovers Vis' and Ramin's flight, he follows them with his army, only to meet a cruel death. Attacked by a wild boar during a night's rest, Mubad chases it on his grey horse and shoots an arrow at the beast, but misses. The boar then throws itself at the king and his horse, dragging them to the ground and tearing the king's body open from chest to navel. With the death of Mubad, Ramin is crowned king of kings. He and Vis happily return to Merv, and they have two sons. When Vis eventually dies, Ramin places her body in an underground tomb and soon joins her there, first handing over the throne and crown to their son Khurshid.

Khusrow and Shirin

The story of Khusrow and Shirin is based on the life of the Sasanian king Khusrow II (Khusrow Parviz). Like the story of Vis and Ramin, the love of Khusrow and Shirin, a Christian princess, has been popular with several poets of later periods. In Firdowsi's *Shahnameh*, however, the love story is a subordinate theme in the life of Khusrow II. By contrast, Nizami makes his late twelfth-century epic revolve around the fortunes and tragedy of the young woman. Nizami wrote his romantic poem one hundred years after the completion of the *Shahnameh*, and his attitude to Firdowsi's work on Khusrow and Shirin is similar to his attitude to the *Iskandarnameh* (*Book of Alexander*). He mentions Firdowsi but regards his account of the two lovers as dry, saying that he will add to the story of their love. And so he does. Nizami's poem is built around the love of Khusrow for Shirin and his struggle to gain her, and Shirin's conflict between her love for Khusrow and her justified fear of being abandoned once he has conquered her. It is interesting that Shirin's mother warns her to remember Vis and not to bring the same degradation and shame upon herself. Other details in Nizami's story, such as Khusrow's passion for another woman followed by his regret and return to Shirin, as well as the long dialogues between the two lovers, are reminiscent of Gurgani's Vis and Ramin, indicating that the poet knew the earlier popular romance but did not regard its story line as morally proper.

Khusrow Parviz, born as son and heir to Hurmuzd IV (AD 579-90), showed remarkable qualities in his early childhood. Not only was his physical beauty striking, but his knowledge and wisdom, courage and power were also unique. He was so skilful with a bow and arrow that he could untie knots and loosen the rings of chain-mail with them. He could bring down lions and make columns fall with his sword. At the age of fourteen he is given into the care of a wise and learned teacher, Buzurg Umid (Buzurg Mihr). Once in a dream his grandfather Anushirvan (Khusrow I Anushirvan) appears to Khusrow and tells the young man that soon he will meet the love of his life; that he will find a new horse called Shabdiz with which not even a storm could keep pace; that he will possess a royal throne; and that he will have a minstrel called Barbad whose art could make even poison taste delicious.

One day Khusrow hears, through his friend Shapur (an accomplished artist), about Mahin Banu and her kingdom near the Caspian Sea. She has a daughter called Shirin (sweet in Persian), whose beauty is like 'a fairy child, a full moonlight'. Her teeth are like pearls, her mouth like ruby. Just hearing about the beauty of the princess makes Khusrow fall in love with her. Shapur plays matchmaker by approaching Shirin when he is in Armenia, showing her a picture of Khusrow. She immediately falls in love with him. Shapur gives her a ring of Khusrow's and tells her to ride to Ctesiphon to join him. The following morning Shirin pretends that she is going hunting and asks her mother for permission to ride Shabdiz, a horse which gallops as fast as the wind. She races off, leaving her followers behind, and rides in the direction of Ctesiphon to find Khusrow. Exhausted at one point in her journey, she halts at a lake, 'the source of life', to bathe. So touching is the image of the beautiful Shirin that the 'sky's eyes filled with tears'.

Meanwhile Khusrow has been in trouble at the royal court in Ctesiphon. A rival king, Bahram Chubin (Bahram VI), has issued coins in the name of Khusrow and circulated them within the kingdom. On this evidence, Hurmuzd believes that his own son is attempting to seize power from him. The wise Buzurg Umid advises Khusrow to leave Ctesiphon for a while, but before he does, he tells his harem at the palace to look out for Shirin and to offer her hospitality and friendship if she arrives. He then rides off in great haste to escape the wrath of his angry father.

As it happens, Khusrow's horses stop to rest at the same place where Shirin is bathing. Khusrow catches a glimpse of her and her fabulous horse from behind the bushes, but is unaware of her identity. When she finally notices him, she wonders who he might be, even asking herself whether it might be Khusrow, as only he is able to stir up such emotions in her. However, she discards this possibility because the man is not wearing royal garb, and she cannot know he is in disguise. Shirin then rides off on Shabdiz and, when Khusrow looks for her again, he cannot find her. He weeps, wishing that he had approached her. Sorrowfully he continues his journey to Armenia while Shirin rides to Ctesiphon. Arriving at the court, she presents herself to the women of the royal harem. Although they immediately resent her charm and beauty, they are none the less obliged to welcome her. Shirin soon discovers Khusrow's flight and becomes convinced that the man she saw while bathing was none other than him. Khusrow meanwhile has reached Armenia, where he is warmly welcomed by Mahin Banu. He stays there for a time, drinking wine and lamenting Shirin's absence.

During Khusrow's stay in Armenia, an envoy is sent to him by a group of noblemen who want him to ascend the throne of Iran, as Khusrow's father Hurmuzd has now died and the country needs its legitimate ruler. Khusrow hurries back to Ctesiphon and is surprised to find Shirin gone. He is told by the women of his harem that she has moved to a palace in the mountains, but in fact she has returned to Armenia with Shapur in the hope of joining Khusrow. On arrival Shirin is greeted only by a joyful mother, pleased to see her daughter back, instead of a loving Khusrow.

Now, however, Khusrow's rightful crown is under threat from his old opponent, Bahram Chubin. The rival king has spread rumours that Khusrow is mad with blind love for Shirin, and he has gained enough support to force Khusrow to flee from Ctesiphon via Azerbaijan to Armenia. Here the two lovers finally meet while out hunting, and they at last declare their love for each other. At this point Mahin Banu advises Shirin not to be carried away by her emotions, cautioning her to insist on becoming Khusrow's legal wife so as not to go down the same path as Vis and her lover Ramin. Shirin finally promises to follow her mother's advice, and tactfully turns aside all Khusrow's passionate advances.

Furious at her seeming rejection, Khusrow leaves Shirin, takes Shabdiz and rides off towards Constantinople (Istanbul). There he marries Maryam, the daughter of the Byzantine emperor, and with the help of the Byzantine army he moves against his opponent Bahram. In a bloody battle Khusrow defeats his rival, who abandons his claim to the throne and escapes to China.

Having won his throne, Khusrow begins once again to think about Shirin. He tries to forget his pain over lost love through the songs of his famous minstrel, Barbad, during festivities at court. Meanwhile, after reminding Shirin of her promise to control her passion for Khusrow, Mahin Banu dies and leaves the crown of Armenia to her daughter.

It is at this point in the story that Farhad appears – a great stonemason renowned for his ability to perform the impossible. When introduced to Shirin, he falls hopelessly in love with her. News of his ardent love soon reaches the ears of Khusrow, who tries to get rid of him, first by offering him gold and then by giving him a never-ending task that will keep him away from the court and from Shirin. After an impassioned dialogue between the two contenders for Shirin's love, Khusrow sets him building a passable route through the mountain of Bisitun in order to facilitate the movement of trading caravans. Farhad agrees on condition that, once the work is completed, Khusrow will give up his claim to Shirin. While Farhad is at work Shirin visits him, bringing him a jug of milk to renew his strength. On the way back, her horse gives way under the heavy weight of her jewellery. But just as the horse and its beautiful rider are about to collapse, Farhad rushes up and lifts both of them on to his shoulders, carrying the mounted Shirin majestically to her palace. When Khusrow hears about this incident and also gets news of Farhad's imminent success in tunnelling through the rock of Bisitun, he realises that he will lose Shirin. He therefore sends a messenger to Farhad, informing him that Shirin has died. Not wishing to live without her, Farhad throws himself off the mountain and dies instantly. This is followed soon after by the death of Khusrow's wife, Maryam.

Khusrow travels to Isfahan, where he falls in love with Shakar (meaning sugar), a girl renowned for her beauty and innocence, and he marries her. But once he has gained sugar (Shakar), which he regards as the body, he yearns for

Illustration from a late 15th-century Khamseh of Nizami, showing Farhad and Shirin meeting at Mount Bisitun. Here, she has given him a jug of milk.

Illustration from a 16th-century Khamseh of Nizami. Shiruy (the historical Kavad II) is about to murder his father Khusrow, who lies beside Shirin.

sweetness (Shirin), which he thinks of as the soul. After an exchange of letters, Khusrow and Shirin listen to a beautiful duet sung by the two court singers, Nakisa and Barbad. Nakisa repeats the words of Shirin and Barbad expresses the feelings of Khusrow. This reconciles the two lovers, and Khusrow promises to marry Shirin. Their love is sealed with a royal wedding, but soon darkness clouds their joy. Shiruy, Khusrow's son by Maryam, falls in love with Shirin when he sees her at his father's wedding. Wanting to marry her himself, Shiruy callously murders Khusrow as he sleeps beside Shirin. But on the day of Khusrow's funeral, Shirin locks herself inside her husband's tomb and kills herself. When her body is discovered, she is ceremoniously laid to rest with Khusrow.

Fairy tales and passion plays

Fairy tales involve supernatural beings, the fairies, whose name comes from the Persian word *pari*. Their origin goes back to the witch-like *pairaka* of the *Avesta*, those wicked forces that were most active during the night. Having the power to change their appearance and turn themselves into beauties, they were able to impose their will on men and use them to do evil. *Paris*, with their great beauty and supernatural powers, play an important role in Persian folklore.

The Thousand and One Nights

One of the most famous collections of ancient tales is *Alf Layla wa Layla*, the Arabic name of *One Thousand Nights and One Night*, commonly known in English as *The Arabian Nights*. These came to Europe during the Middle Ages but were not written down in a European language until the beginning of the eighteenth century, when Antoine Galland translated them into French. Translations into English by Edward Lane and Sir Richard Burton followed in the nineteenth century.

Best known for stories such as *Ali Baba and the Forty Thieves*, *The Adventures of Sinbad* and *Aladdin and the Magic Lamp*, this collection is not a homogenous group but a miscellany with origins in different cultures, some of them very ancient. One of the many lands that has contributed stories to this collection is ancient Persia, and other tales can be traced to India, Greece, Egypt, Arabia, ancient Mesopotamia and Turkey, making the original title of *One Thousand Nights and One Night* more appropriate than simply *The Arabian Nights*.

Sources dating to the tenth century ad which mention this collection allude to the existence of a Persian book called *Hazar afsaneh* (*The Book of a Thousand Tales*), the story of a king, his vizier, and the vizier's daughters Shahrazad and Dinazad. These same characters appear in the story that frames *One Thousand Nights and One Night*, though here the main plot is built around two brothers, the Sasanian kings Shahzaman and Shahriyar, one of whom rules in Samarkand and the other in India and China. Both find out that their wives have been unfaithful, and all the women and slaves involved in their affairs are beheaded. Shahriyar then decides to take a new young bride every night and to have her beheaded in the morning. However, after three years have passed, it is becoming impossible for the king's vizier to find any more young girls for his master. At this point the vizier's own daughter Shahrazad persuades her father to let her go to the king, taking her younger sister Dinazad with her. As part of her plan she instructs Dinazad to ask her for a story every night, and she is then able to make them last for one thousand and one nights by always breaking off at a crucial point, thereby arousing the king's interest in hearing the rest of the story the following night.

During this period Shahrazad gives birth to three male children by the king, and when her storytelling finally ends he offers to grant her a wish. She asks the king to spare her life for the sake of their young children, which he willingly agrees to do, and they live happily ever after.

The names of Shahriyar (holder of a kingdom; prince or king), Shahrazad (Chihrazad, meaning of noble lineage) and Dinazad (exalting the goddess Den) are Iranian, and the name of Shahriyar's brother Shahzaman consists of the Persian *shah* (king) and Arabic *zaman* (time). It is believed that the frame story of *One Thousand Nights and One Night* is of both Persian and Indian origin.

Among the tales in the collection which are believed to be of Persian origin are love stories and fairy tales, which often include *div* and *pari* as well as magical animals and birds. Other stories, such as *The Ebony Horse*, although beginning with a description which fits perfectly into the Persian tradition, are nevertheless believed to be of Indian origin. *The Ebony Horse*, also known as *The Magic Horse*, is about a magical horse presented as a gift to the king of Persia.

> There was in ancient times, in the country of the Persians, a mighty King, of great dignity, who had three daughters, like shining full moons and flowery gardens; and he had a male child, like the moon. He observed two annual festivals, that of the New Year's day, and that of the Autumnal Equinox; and it was his custom, on these occasions, to open his palaces, and give his gifts . . . the people of his dominions also used to go in to him and salute him, and congratulate him on the festival, offering him presents and servants . . .

The king's young heir sits on the ebony horse to test the magic and flies into the sky. He visits another country (Yemen), falls in love with a princess, and after a series of adventures returns to his father's court and marries the princess.

The story of Hasan of el-Basra

This story concerns a wealthy merchant of the city of Basra who has two sons. After his death, the brothers divide their father's wealth between them. One opens a copperware shop and the other works as a goldsmith.

> Now while the goldsmith was sitting in his shop, one day, lo, a Persian walked along the market-street among the people until he came to the shop of the young goldsmith . . . And the name of the young goldsmith was Hasan . . .

The Persian finds Hasan looking at a mysterious old book. He tells the young goldsmith that he alone in the world knows an art that can bring untold wealth, and he says that he is willing to teach Hasan this art because he has no son of his own. 'To-morrow I will corne to thee, and will make for thee, of copper, pure gold in thy presence.'

When Hasan goes home and tells his mother about his visitor she warns him not to trust the Persian, but he takes no notice of her. The next day the Persian magically produces a lump of precious gold from base copper, and Hasan sells it in the market for fifteen thousand pieces of silver. The following day Hasan persuades the Persian to come home with him and teach him the art of alchemy. After some successful experiments, the alchemist tells Hasan that he wants him to marry his daughter and then gives him what looks like a sweetmeat. This causes Hasan to fall unconscious, upon which the alchemist gleefully bundles him and all his family treasures into two trunks and goes out to call a porter. They then sail away on a ship.

The Persian is, in fact, Bahram, the *magian* (Zoroastrian priest) who slaughters a Muslim once a year. During the sea voyage, the *magian* takes Hasan out of the trunk, 'poured some vinegar into his nostrils, and blew a powder into his nose . . .' The duped goldsmith regains consciousness and, realising what has happened to him, immediately thinks of his mother's warning. The *magian* tries to convert Hasan to Zoroastrianism, but as a devout Muslim he resists, despite being beaten and suffering greatly. When the sea suddenly becomes rough and the winds howl, the crew know it is the work of God: the *magian* stops torturing Hasan and the stormy weather abates at once. He then regrets what he has done and 'swore to the fire and the light' that he will no longer torture Hasan.

The two are thus reconciled and their voyage continues for three months in the direction of ' the Mountain of the Clouds, on which is the elixir with which we practise alchemy'. Once on land, they mount camels and ride to the top of a high mountain where, according to the *magian*, a special herb necessary to perform alchemy is to be found. There once again he plays a trick on Hasan, abandoning him on the top of the mountain. Hasan plunges into the sea on the other side of the mountain, hoping that God will either put ari end to his misfortune or help him. By divine intervention, the waves carry him ashore, and from there he sees a palace, already described to him by the *magian* as the residence of demons and evil creatures. But Hasan does not believe his words and, indeed, when he enters the palace he finds two beautiful young women playing chess. They rejoice greatly to see him alive after they hear his story about the wicked *magian*, the enchanter.

The two princesses and their five sisters have been placed in this isolated palace by their father, a king, and Hasan stays with them for a year. Then one day, while out fishing, he sees the *magian* approaching with a new victim. He and the princesses manage to kill the *magian* and rescue the captive young man.

Later the king comes to take his daughters to a marriage celebration, which will keep them away for two months. They tell Hasan, who has been hidden from the king, to remain in the palace during their absence. They also entrust him with the key to a locked room but warn him never to open it. However, boredom and curiosity overcome him, and one day he opens the forbidden door. After climbing some stairs that lead to a roof, he sees a pool and garden filled with amazing birds and other creatures. There is also a group of beautiful fairy-like girls bathing in the pool and, as he watches them, he loses his senses incomplete enchantment.

When the sisters return, one of them finds Hasan hiding in his room, in a state of sorrow and shock, having fallen in love with one of the bewitching bathers. He is told that his beloved is the daughter of a powerful king, and that she comes to the pool once a month at new moon. Hasan waits for the next new moon, goes to the pool and sees the princess arrive with her sisters disguised in a bird's costume. On leaving the pool, the princess cannot find her costume, which Hasan has hidden, and her weeping sisters must leave her behind. Hasan then takes the princess to his room by force and locks her in, and eventually she agrees to marry him.

One night Hasan has a dream in which he sees his mother weeping, and he decides to return to her with his wife, promising the seven princesses of the palace that he will visit them regularly. After a long journey, they reach his home. His poor mother, who has giyen up hope of ever seeing her son again, is overjoyed and welcomes his new wife and their two small children. Hasan then decides to move to Baghdad and they setup home there.

When the time comes for him to visit the seven princesses, he entrusts his wife and children to his mother's care, warning her that under no circumstances should she let his young wife leave the house or see the bird's costume which he has hidden in a trunk. Hasan's wife overhears their conversation and, once her husband has left, she begs her mother-in-law to allow her to go to the baths. The old woman finally gives in. While bathing, the beautiful wife is seen by a slave of one of the caliph's wives, who rushes to her mistress to tell her of the fairy-like beauty of Hasan's wife. The slave warns that if the caliph sees her, he will not be able to suppress his desire to have her. A slave is then sent to Hasan's house to bring his mother and wife to the caliph's palace. Hasan's wife tells the caliph's wife about her extraordinary dress of feathers and how it is being hidden from her. Hasan's mother at first denies it, but then is forced to hand over the dress. Hasan's wife puts it on, enfolds the two children inside it, and fastens it. She then turns into a bird and flies into the air. Hasan's mother, weeping and wailing in desperation, asks what she should tell her son. His wife shouts down to her from above that if he wants her, he will have to follow her to the islands of Wak-Wak. She then disappears in the distance.

When Hasan returns home and finds his wife and children gone, he is heartbroken, but then resolves to return to the palace of the seven sisters and ask for their help. They tell him that their uncle is the only one who can help him, which he does through magic and with the assistance of supernatural beings, and Hasan eventually reaches the islands of Wak-Wak. There he meets an old woman who feels sorry for him after hearing his story, and she leads him to the queen of one of the islands. Hasan is amazed at the queen's resemblance to his missing wife, who is in fact her sister. Angry with her sister for marrying Hasan without asking permission from their father, she has in fact decided to punish her and the two children by putting them all to death; Even this is overcome, however, and again through the intervention of the Almighty and various

Illustration from an 18th-century Kashmiri abridged prose Shahnameh showing the execution of Siyavush. His head is cut off and later a tree springs from his spilled blood.

supernatural forces Hasan manages to escape with his wife (who,
supernatural forces Hasan manages to escape with his wife (who,
incidentally, is overjoyed to see him), their children and the sympathetic old woman. They return to the palace of the seven sisters and from there go back to Baghdad, where they are reunited with Hasan's mother.

The passion plays

The passion plays are written around the martyrdom of holy figures. The best-known ancient saga about the martyrdom of an Iranian prince is that of Siyavush, son of Kay Kavus, who is brutally murdered by Afrasiyab, the king of Turan (described in great detail by Firdowsi in the *Shahnameh*). His death is seen as especially tragic because Siyavush has only gone to live at Afrasiyab's court in order to escape his stepmother's jealousy and his father's suspicion, and because his murder leaves his wife Farangis, daughter of Afrasiyab, five months pregnant (with Kay Khusrow, the future king of Iran). Siyavush foresees his own tragic end in a dream and tells Farangis that he will be beheaded; that there will be no coffin, no grave and no shroud for him; that no one will mourn him.

On hearing the news of Siyavush's death, his father, the king of Iran, weeps and tears his clothes, and heroes such as Tus, Gudarz, Giv, Gurgin and others don black garments. Rustam faints with sorrow and officially mourns for a week. He then swears to avenge Siyavush's murder by destroying Afrasiyab and turning Turan into a river of blood.

The mourning of Siyavush (*sug-i Siyavush*) as described by Firdowsi is thus the mourning of the Iranian people for their beloved young prince, victim of a conspiracy. His loss is turned into an emotional story which has acquired a prominent place in the *Shahnameh*.

The myth of Siyavush is of ancient Iranian origin and his name (Siyavarshan) is frequently mentioned in the *Avesta*. The mourning of Siyavush was already a well-known custom in Central Asia in the tenth century AD, celebrated in song. It is further reported that people in Sogdia mourned Siyavush once a year by striking their faces and offering food and drink to the dead.

The perpetuation in Islamic times of this emotional mourning tradition surrounding the slaying of a martyr is best seen in the passion plays (*ta'ziyeh*) of the Shiite Muslims, in which the murder and martyrdom of Imam Husayn and his family, grandson of the prophet Muhammad, are mourned in the Muslim month of Muharram (first month of the lunar calendar). The historical facts behind this tragedy begin with the death of the prophet Muhammad in AD 632 and the subsequent split in the Muslim community between those who favoured succession by election (the Sunnis) and succession through inheritance from the prophet (the Shiites). Ali, the son-in-law of the prophet and the fourth caliph to succeed him, was seen by the Shiites as the legitimate successor. After both he and his eldest son Imam Hasan were assassinated, the Sunni governor Yezid became the caliph and moved his capital to Damascus. Husayn, Ali's younger son, the legitimate successor in the eyes of the Shiites, was encouraged by the people of Kufa to revolt against the caliphate and to fight for the right of rule by the house of Ali. On his way to Kufa, Husayn and his followers met Yezid and

Illustration from an 18th-century Kashmiri abridged prose Shahnameh. The young prince Kay Khusrow and his mother Farangis (disguised as a man, but without a beard) follow Giv across the River Jayhun (Oxus, Amu Darya) to go from Turan to Iran.

his vast army on the plains of Kerbela, south-west of Baghdad. Husayn, his family and his followers survived ten days in the desert without water but were finally brutally murdered by Yezid and his army. The desert ordeal began on the first day of Muharram and the bloody murder took place on the tenth (the *Ashura*).

Mourning processions already existed in the tenth century AD and were common in the city of Baghdad at the time. Under the rule of the Safavids in Iran in the sixteenth century and with the establishment of Shiite Islam as the official state religion, the mourning ceremonies of Muharram officially incorporated the passion plays, the *ta'ziyeh*. The tradition reached its peak at the end of the nineteenth and beginning of the twentieth century, although it is still intact today.

Professional actors, all men, played throughout the year and in particular during Muharram, performing either in the mosque, the *bazar* (covered market) or in a special building, the *takiyeh*. The most famous of these, the *Takiyeh Dowlat*, built in Tehran under the royal patronage of the Qajar king Nasiruddin Shah in 1869, was modelled on the Albert Hall in London. A large audience of several thousand would gather at the *takiyeh*, following the passion plays about Imam Husayn and his family with great excitement. Often, too, there would be stories of the life and deeds of other Shiite martyrs. Once again, the continuation of an ancient tradition, the mourning ritual, has its roots in the traditions of the distant past. The *sug-i Siyavush* was replaced by the mourning of Imam Husayn and other Shiite martyrs.

Edward Browne, one of the great scholars of Iranian studies, described the passion plays as 'heart-moving'. He quotes the *ta'ziyeh* of Bibi Shahrbanu, legendary daughter of the last Sasanian king, Yazdigird III (633–51), who became the wife of the martyred Imam Husayn. Because of the myth of her Iranian ancestry, she is particularly popular among Persians:

> Born of the race of Yazdigird the King
> From Nushirwan my origin I trace.
> What time kind Fortune naught but joy did bring
> In Ray's proud city was my home and place.
> There in my father's palace once at night
> In sleep to me came Fatima 'the Bright';
> 'O Shahr-banu' – thus the vision cried –
> 'I give thee to Husayn to be his bride!'
> Said I, 'Behold Mada'in is my home,
> And how shall I to far Madina roam?
> Impossible!' But Fatima cried, 'Nay,
> Husayn shall hither come in war's array
> And bear thee hence, a prisoner of war,
> From this Mada'in to Madina far,
> Where, joined in wedlock with Husayn, my boy,
> Thou shalt bear children who will be my joy.
> For nine Imams to thee shall owe their birth,
> The like of whom hath not been seen on earth!'

Conclusion

The myths and legends of Iran, the Persian myths, reflect the survival of an ancient tradition in the culture as well as the language of a large geographical area extending beyond the political boundaries of modern Iran. Neither nomadic movements, invasions nor internal political changes and upheavals have succeeded in destroying the ancient sagas; on the contrary, these legends have survived for millennia. Their preservation has kept alive the traditions and social concepts of a distant past and at the same time helped the Persian language and literature to survive and develop.

Persian myths were primarily passed on through oral transmission and it was only in later periods, mainly under the Parthians and Sasanians, that many of the stories were written down. These myths, some of pagan and others of Zoroastrian origin, survived the Arab conquest in the seventh century and the adoption of the new faith of Islam. The works of such great poets as Daqiqi and Firdowsi enabled people to read or listen to these stories in their own language and not merely through Arabic translations. There is an abundance of such books (*namehs*) in Persian literature, but Firdowsi's *Shahnameh* occupies a special and unique position because of the beauty and clarity of its language. The heroes of the *Shahnameh*, Rustam, Sohrab and Isfandiyar, are part of the life of every Iranian, and to this day it is common practice to read and recite their stories.

Shahnameh khani, reading the *Book of Kings*, is a special art performed by professional storytellers (*naqqal*) in towns and villages. The *naqqal* puts on a one-man act, reciting tragic and heroic stories. Rustam, the hero of all heroes, is a particular favourite, and his adventures and combats are performed for appreciative audiences of all ages. Through gesticulation and a combination of poetry recitation and singing, the *naqqal* carries his listeners with him from battle-field to royal court, making them laugh with his mimicry and reducing them to tears with moving descriptions of poignant and brutal murders. These stories are often interrupted at crucial points and continued the following day, thus stretching one story over several days.

Persian myths have not only played an important role in Persian literature, but mythological scenes depicting heroes and anti-heroes have also entered the world of visual art. Since at least the fourteenth century, illustrated manuscripts of the *Shahnameh* have included such myths and legends. The snake-shouldered Zahhak, Fariydun and his bull-headed mace, the invincible Isfandiyar, the lion-like Rustam, the guardian bird Simurgh and the *div* have all become familiar

'Coffee house' painting of Rustam holding his dying son Sohrab in his arms. The amulet that once belonged to Rustam is visible under Sohrab's torn sleeve. The armies of Iran and Turan face each other in the background, as do the horses of the heroes. Beside Rakhsh lies Rustam's bull-headed mace. The larger oil painting dates from the middle of this century.

figures in Persian paintings. Stories from the Rustam saga were popular for the decoration of tiles. By the end of the nineteenth and the beginning of the twentieth century a genre of paintings by folk artists, the so-called *qahveh khaneh* (coffee house) paintings, were also reproducing scenes from the *Shahnameh*. In all these ways, Persian myths continue to prove their relevance to the beliefs, social attitudes and tastes of the Iranian people today.

Suggestions for further reading

Perhaps one of the most fascinating aspects of Persian myths is the fact that they have survived into modern Persian literature and language. There is therefore a very wide range of sources, covering several millennia, and the myths are closely related to the history and archaeology of ancient Iran.

The most valuable and informative source for the religion of the ancient Iranians is Mary Boyce, *A History of Zoroastrianism* in three volumes (Leiden, Koln, 1975, 1982, 1991). English translations of Zoroastrian sacred texts appear in the series *Sacred Books of the East*, edited by Max Müller, and they include J. Darmesteter, *The Zend Avesta* in three volumes (Delhi, 1974, 1975) and E. W. West, *The Pahlavi Texts* (Delhi, 1970). *Persian Mythology* by John R. Hinnells (New York, 1985) examines in detail Zoroastrian and pre-Zoroastrian myths and their significance in modern Zoroastrianism. Ehsan Yarshater, in an article on 'Iranian Historical Tradition' ,in the *Cambridge History of Iran*, III, I (Cambridge, 1983), pp. 343ff, analyses the beliefs of the ancient Iranians and provides a detailed bibliography of ancient and modern sources. This is supplemented by entries in the invaluable *Encyclopedia Iranica* (also edited by E. Yarshater), published in New York since 1985. For an overview of different aspects of Zoroastrianism, see Pheroza J. Godrej and Firoza Puntakey Mistree, *A Zoroastrian Tapestry: Art, Religion and Culture* (Bombay, 2002).

English translations of the *Shahnameh* include the version in verse by Arthur George and Edmund Warner, *The Shahnama of Firdausi* in ten volumes (London, 1905-25). For prose translations see Reuben Levy, *The Epic of the Kings* (London, Boston, 1977) and Jerome F. Clinton, *The Tragedy of Sohrab and Rostam* (Seattle, London, 1987). Important articles on the *Shahnameh* and related topics have been published in the periodical *Iranshenasi* in Persian, but with an English resumé. Also informative are articles in the *Encyclopaedia of Islam* (Leiden, new edition 1960–), and a recent bibliography of Firdowsi has been prepared by A. Shapur Shahbazi, *Firdowsi: A Critical Bibliography* (Costa Mesa, California, 1991).

The original Persian sources themselves exist in a large number of editions which cannot be listed here. It is worth noting, however, that a recent edition of *The Shahnameh* by Djalal Khaleghi Motlagh was published in 1988 and 1990 in New York. The edition used in the present volume was published in Tehran in 1975/6. Other Persian works that have been consulted include Nizami's *Khusrow o Shirin* and *Iskandarnameh in Kulliyat-e Khamseh-ye Hakim Nizami Ganjavi* (Tehran, 1991/2) and Gurgani, *Vis o Ramin* (Tehran, 1971). Publications by Iranian scholars on Persian mythology in Persian include S. Safa, *Hamaseh sara-yi dar Iran* (Tehran, 1984/5) and M. Bahar, *Asatir-e Iran* (Tehran, 1973/4). For the importance and position of storytellers and particularly minstrels in the Iranian tradition, see Mary Boyce, 'The Parthian gosan and Iranian minstrel tradition', in *Journal of the Royal Asiatic Society* (1957), pp. 10ff. E. W. Lane gives an English translation of *1001 Nights* in *The Arabian Nights' Entertainments* (London, 1898), and a detailed examination of the stories appears in Mia Gerhardt, *The Art of Story Telling* (Leiden, 1963). The tradition and development of the *ta'ziyeh*, the passion plays, are dealt with in Peter J. Chelkowski (ed.), *Ta'ziyeh: Ritual and Drama in Iran* (New York, 1979). A useful and informative overview of Persian literature can be found in Edward G. Browne, *A Literary History of Persia* (London, 1909).

For the history and archaeology of Iran in the pre-Islamic period, see Richard N. Frye, *History of Ancient Iran* (Munich, 1984), Georgina Herrmann, *The Iranian Revival* (Oxford, 1977, John Curtis, *Ancient Persia* (2nd edn, London, 2000) and Josef Wiesehofer, *Ancient Persia* (London, 2001).

Index and picture credits

References in italics indicate illustrations

Picture credits

Front cover: Reproduced by kind permission of the Collection of the Aga Khan, *pp. 4–5:* Warwick Ball; *p. 9:* BM WAA 1992–1–25.1; *p. 12:* BM WAA 123267; *p. 15:* BM WAA 124093; *p. 16:* BM GR 1825.6–13.1 (Sculpture 1720); *p. 17:* BM (CM) P. R. Knight Collection II. AI, p. 202; *p. 18:* Warwick Ball; *p. 20:* BM WAA 135913; *p. 22:* BM WAA 124095; *p. 23:* BM WAA 124092; *p. 25:* Trustees of the British Library, Or371, f. 7r; *p. 27:* BM WAA 134963; *p. 30:* BM OA 1943.10–9.02; *p. 31:* BL Or371, f. 8r; *p. 33:* BL Or371, f. 17r; *p. 35: (top)* BM OA 1948.12–11.020; *(bottom)* BL Or371, f. 24v; *p. 38:* BL Or371, f. 35r; *p. 39:* BL Or8761, f. 52v; *p. 40:* BM OA 1975.5–23.02; *p. 42:* BM OA 1922.7–11.02; *p. 43:* BM OA 1948.12–11.025; *p. 45:* BM OA 1928.12–6.01; *p. 46: (top)* BL Or371, f. 48r; *(bottom)* BM OA 1975.5–23.03; *p. 48:* BL Or11522, f. 123v; *p. 49:* BL Or371, f. 178r; *p. 50: (top)* BM OA 1937.7–10.0327; *(bottom)* BM OA 1975.5–23.04; *p. 52:* BM OA 1920.9–17.051; *p. 55:* BM WAA 90920; *p. 57:* BL Or2834, f. 266v; *p. 59:* BM CM 1919–8–20–1; *p. 61:* BL Or2265, f. 77v; *p. 63:* BM WAA 93028; *p. 64:* Hermitage, St Petersburg; *p. 68:* BL Or2834, f. 70v; *p. 69:* BL Or2932, f. 110v; *p. 74:* BL Or8761, f. 115v; *p. 75:* BL Or371, f. 105v; *p. 78:* Reza Abbasi Museum, Tehran; *chapter motif:* Vesta Curtis (after BM WAA 124095)